Jigsaw2

ACKNOWLEDGEMENTS:

Jigsaw 2 was originally written for overseas work, based on themes and session titles by Janet Richards.
   Material selected for this book was contributed by Alison Ball, Ian Copeman, Dinah Davis,
   Peter Empson, Lindsay Fogwill, Catriona Foster, Miriam Harvey, Priscilla Hodson, Stuart Holt,
   Pam Jarrett, Jill Luce, Kath Pickersgill, Kate Ross, Jane Sutton, Anne Taylor, Pam Weaver,
   Alison Webber, Elaine Williams and Michelle Williams;
Priscilla Hodson and Elaine Williams then revised, adapted and added to the material;
Matthew Slater did the typesetting, artwork and design;
and it was checked by John Chapman!

Printed and bound in the United Kingdom by Stanley L Hunt (Printers) Ltd, Rushden, Northants.

Scriptures quoted from the New Century Version (Anglicised Edition) copyright © 1993 by
   Nelson Word Ltd, 9 Holdom Avenue, Bletchley, Milton Keynes, MK1 1QR, UK. (One verse quoted from
   the Contemporary English Version, copyright © American Bible Society 1991, 1992, 1995.)

Crusaders, 2 Romeland Hill, ST ALBANS, Herts, AL3 4ET. Tel: (01727) 855422

Contents

The Jigsaw Project has been designed to help you communicate key Christian truths to youngsters growing up in a variety of different social, cultural and family situations.

Introduction

Jigsaw 2 contains 36 <u>more</u> short, straightforward and easy-to-prepare teaching outlines to fit into a club programme. The material is particularly geared to outreach work with youngsters between the ages of 7 and 13... but you could also use it as a basis for teaching in other groups.

Each session outline follows the same pattern:-

> **BIBLE BASE**
> - the key passage <u>or</u> verses!

> **WE WANT OUR YOUNGSTERS TO...**
> - the teaching points to bring out of the session;

> **LEAD-IN***
> - an activity to 'set the scene';

> **HOW TO START***
> - a framework to help you teach the main points - please see **Guidelines 1** for more help with this!

> **ACTIVITIES***
> - a choice of <u>TWO</u> activities which link in with or build on the theme - although they appear at the end of the outline, it may sometimes be best to run them before your main teaching;

> **KEY VERSE**

> **A PAGE FOR YOUR OWN NOTES WHICH MAY BE HELPFUL...**

> (* The symbols ➤ ◀ in these sections denote things you will need to do in advance!)

● **YOU can go through the themes in any order, but the sessions within a theme do tend to follow on from each other;**

● **YOU can keep the sessions together in this book... <u>or</u> tear them out along the perforated lines, give them to your co-leaders to prepare, then keep them in a folder afterwards;**

● **YOU will need to select and adapt the material according to the interests of the youngsters in your group;**

and, most importantly,

● **YOU will always need to pray for God's guidance and direction as you prepare to lead each session!**

1. Developing HOW TO START

From the basic framework in each HOW TO START section, you can:

Guidelines
1

A. **Tell the rest of the story from a Bible story book...** It's worth investing in one which goes through the whole Bible, such as *The Lion Children's Bible* (Lion), *The Lion Storyteller Bible* (Lion) or *The Children's Illustrated Bible* (Dorling Kindersley);

B. **Prepare to re-tell the whole story** or **present the message in your own words.**

When you are speaking...

- ✔ **practise beforehand**. Be familiar with what you are going to say: it always sounds 'flat' if you read straight from a book or your notes, and it makes eye-contact impossible!
- ✔ **vary the tone and pace of your voice** to go with what you are saying;
- ✔ **introduce different voice types,** (eg for men, women, children, older people etc), but only if you can do them well!

But remember... don't just talk!

Many youngsters find it difficult to learn by when they only listen, so:

* *add visuals*: there are specific suggestions in many sessions - but you can also try them in others! Possibilities include:
- ○ performing a **drama** for your youngsters to watch;
- ○ showing a **video**;
- ○ showing **OHP pictures** - draw your own or trace them from a book;
- ○ showing **comic strip-style stories** - even simple pin people can be expressive!
- ○ moving figures and scenes on **metal** or **flannelboard**;
- ○ using **puppets;**
- ○ showing **artefacts** ...and so on.

* *get your youngsters to be as active as possible!* Again, there are specific suggestions in some sessions. Possibilities include:
- ○ **discussion** - talk together about feelings, reactions and opinions, (eg how do you think he/she feels? What do you think he/she should do now? What do you think is going to happen next? What do you think about ...? and so on);
- ○ **art** - have your youngsters sketch the action or the expressions on someone's face as you tell a story;
- ○ **drama** - have your youngsters act out or mime the action as you tell it ...and so on.

C. **Occasionally use the passage straight from the Bible...** but only if you check first that it does not contain words and ideas which will be lost on your youngsters! And make sure that you use a good clear, modern version such as the Contemporary English, Good News or New Century versions.

During this part of your programme, always aim to:

- ✔ **be well-prepared...**
- ✔ **keep it fast-moving...** disruption is more likely if your youngsters get bored!
- ✔ **make it varied...** try different ideas and approaches!
- ✔ **let your youngsters know what is expected from them...** it's good to involve them in setting the boundaries right at the outset, (eg 'only one person talks at a time', 'we respect what others do and say', etc). You may have to negotiate, (eg in setting a time limit for the teaching slot - and not overrunning!)
- ✔ **be confident!** After all, if God is with us, we don't need to feel fearful... (*2 Timothy 1:7*)!

2. Working with Youngsters in 1990's Britain

Guidelines 2

○ **Be open about what you do and believe as a Christian.**

○ **Know about the faiths of the youngsters in your group. Also, be aware of things which could cause embarrassment and offence:**

 ! **never put Bibles, any Bible verses you have written out or songbooks on the floor - some youngsters will think that you have no respect for God or for His Word;**

 ! **don't insist that someone reads out loud from the Bible, prays out loud or takes part in a dramatisation of a Bible story;**

 ! **if you are making something with a Bible verse written on it, don't insist that the youngsters take it home;**

 ! **if you are having food or cooking as an activity, make sure that you cater for everyone, (eg pork is forbidden to youngsters from a Muslim background).**

○ **Make sure that any pictures or artefacts are multi-cultural.**

○ **Support the way the youngsters are being brought up as far as possible.** Try to visit them at home. Every now and then, organise an activity which involves the parents.

○ **Be aware of the family situations of your youngsters.** Avoid talking as if everyone comes from one particular family type, (eg has both parents living at home).

○ **Enjoy the fact that your youngsters come from different backgrounds.** It's really interesting to compare and contrast traditions. Don't feel threatened if youngsters speak in their own language (but it is helpful if you can learn to pick up when they start swearing!)

○ **Be sensitive to youngsters who have difficulties with reading and writing.** Never force anyone to read out loud. Where reading is essential, try to pair non-readers with someone who can read.

○ **Deal decisively with any discriminatory comments and behaviour.** You may also need to watch out for this as the youngsters arrive and leave the premises. Help the youngsters concerned understand why this is not right.

○ **Keep going!** Even when it gets tough, remember that God <u>is</u> at work in the lives of your youngsters:

[The LORD says:] "Rain and snow fall from the sky and don't return without watering the ground. They cause the plants to sprout and grow, making seeds fro the farmer and bread for the people. The same thing is true of the words I speak. They will not return to me empty. They make the things happen that I want to happen, and they succeed in doing what I send them to do."

Isaiah 55:10-11

Checklist

☐ _____
☐ _____
☐ _____
☐ _____
☐ _____
☐ _____

Date _____

Planning Notes

Things to remember for next time...

TITLE: A Very Special Book!

The Bible 1 of 1

BIBLE BASE: Select from **Psalm 19:9-11, Psalm 119:105, Jeremiah 23:29, 2 Timothy 3:16, Hebrews 4:12, James 1:23-25 & 1 Peter 2:2**

WE WANT OUR YOUNGSTERS TO...

- ... know that the stories they hear at your club are very special because they come from the Bible;
- ... understand that God speaks to us in the Bible.

LEAD-IN: ➤ In advance, guess how many people will be at your session: cut some magazine pictures <u>or</u> old birthday cards <u>or</u> old posters into that number of small pieces. ◀ Begin by showing the prize! Then hand out all the pieces... and just say 'go'! There should be confusion as everyone complains that they don't know what to do! Use this to bring out how important instructions are. Link in with the idea that the Bible is a set of instructions for all of life! Finish by giving the instructions for the game: the first group to put together a whole picture wins the prize. And run the game!

HOW TO START:
[Have a Bible on show as you do this!]

- ◆ ➤ In advance, collect together objects to go with the word pictures found in the verses above, (ie a lamp, a mirror etc). ◀ Keep the objects hidden...
- ◆ Begin: ***God really wants <u>us</u> to know what He is like, how we can know Him and how we can live right. So He asked people to write down true stories, poems, His laws, good advice, visions about the future... We can find <u>all</u> of these things in just one book - the Bible! God really does speak to <u>us</u> when we hear stories and teaching from the Bible...***
- ◆ ...Reveal the objects one by one - bring out very simply (and briefly!) how each is like the Bible!

ACTIVITIES:

1. Bible Exploration

➤ In advance, send each of your youngsters **individually** a short written message. In it, <u>either</u> ask them to bring an important piece of news that they see, read or hear about; <u>Or</u> something which contains information <u>and/or</u> a story, (eg a magazine, newspaper, poem, song, map, post card, letter etc) - try to ask everyone for something different! (<u>Alternatively</u>, get these things together yourself.) ◀ Talk together about the different ways in which we get information and stories. Then, as appropriate, make links with books in the Bible, (eg a letter with Romans, a song with Psalms etc).

2. Bible Advertisement

Ask your youngsters to get into small groups. Ask each group to design an advert to tell people about the Bible - they could make posters <u>or</u> script and act out an advert for radio <u>or</u> TV. Suggest that they use some of the word pictures from the Bible verses. Have an opportunity to see everyone's ideas!

Extra: As appropriate, also display Bibles and Bible text in as many forms as you can (including cassette, video and CD-ROM?) - encourage your youngsters to look!

KEY VERSE: *All Scripture is given by God and is useful for teaching, for showing people what is wrong in their lives, for correcting faults and for teaching how to live right.*
2 Timothy 3:16

Checklist

- [ ]
- [ ]
- [ ]
- [ ]
- [ ]
- [ ]

Planning Notes

Things to remember for next time...

TITLE: Proud Boy

BIBLE BASE: **Genesis 37:1-11** (Joseph the Dreamer)

WE WANT OUR YOUNGSTERS TO...

... understand that God knows the future;
... consider that He has special plans for their lives.

LEAD-IN: Come to the club dressed unusually!
➤ Also, in advance, collect together some items of significant clothing, (eg a uniform, something for a special occasion, something from the past etc). ◄ As you show them, ask: **what do these clothes tell you about the person wearing them?**

HOW TO START:
◆ ➤ In advance, draw 12 simple figures. Also, cut out a coat-shape to stick on one of the figures from special coloured paper <u>or</u> cloth. ◄
◆ Say that the 12 figures are brothers who worked on the land...
◆ ...Have some youngsters draw and colour suitable clothes on each of the figures.
◆ Then add the special coat to one of them - ask: **what difference does this coat make? What might the other brothers think of it?**
◆ Use this to lead in to the story: ***Joseph's brothers cringed as he went by. The coat his dad gave him was supposed to make him special, but it only made his brothers hate him more...***

ACTIVITIES: 1. 'Shine like Stars'

<u>Either</u> altogether <u>or</u> in small groups with a leader, ask your youngsters: **what do you want to do in the future?** Try to listen to everyone's hopes, ambitions and fears. Talk about God having special plans for <u>**everyone**</u>. Share something from your own life, as appropriate. Then have your youngsters make a star from card and colour it <u>or</u> cover it with foil. <u>Either</u> add them all to a dark background <u>or</u> hang them separately with lengths of sewing cotton. Link in with the KEY VERSE: use the stars to illustrate the idea that God's plan is for us to make a real difference in our world!

2. **Clothes Relay**

Get together a large pile of clothes - the more unusual, the better! Ask your youngsters to get into two teams. Put the pile of clothes at one end of your meeting room and the two teams at the other! On the word 'go', the first person from each team runs and grabs one item from the pile. He/she puts it on, runs back to the team and the second person runs. Continue like this until everybody is wearing something from the pile. The fastest team to do this, wins!

Extra: You could teach some of the songs from the musical, 'Joseph and His Amazing Technicolour Dreamcoat'! 'Joseph's Dream' fits in with this session.

KEY VERSE: *... you shine like stars in the dark world.* Philippians 2:15

Checklist

☐ ....
☐ ....
☐ ....
☐ ....
☐ ....
☐ ....

Date ....

Planning Notes

Things to remember for next time...

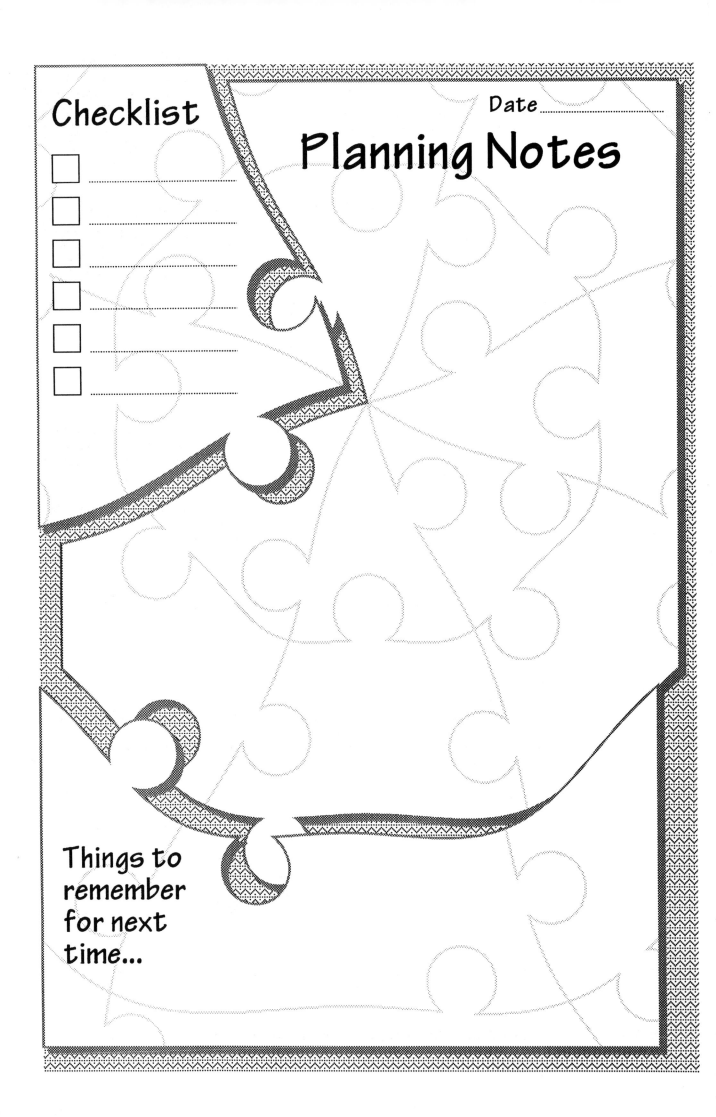

TITLE: Slave

BIBLE BASE: **Genesis 37:12-36 & 39:1-5**
(Joseph Sold into Slavery & Joseph is
Sold to Potiphar)

WE WANT OUR YOUNGSTERS TO...
  ... **know that, even if things get bad, God
  is always there!**
  ... **learn that, even in difficult situations,
  it's important to do your best.**

LEAD-IN:
Ask your youngsters to get into teams of about six.
Give each team some newspaper (or similar) and some sticky tape or glue or
paper clips. Show everyone how to make a simple paper chain with strips of
paper. Now ask for a volunteer from each team. Challenge each team to turn its
volunteer into a 'slave' with paper chains round the wrists and ankles. Talk
briefly together about what this would be like for real...

HOW TO START:
◆ Begin: *"Where have they gone to?" said Joseph to himself. He seemed to
   have been walking for hours, but there was still no sign of his brothers as
   he scanned the horizon. Hidden in the valley below, one brother looked up
   wearily and rubbed his eyes. "Look who it is", he groaned, "I'd recognise
   that coat anywhere..."*
◆ Stop the story when Joseph is sold into Potiphar's household - explain simply
   and briefly what life as a slave would have been like...
◆ ...Ask: **what do you think Joseph is going to do now?**
◆ Explain that Joseph actually worked really hard and earned a promotion: he
   knew that God was with him!
◆ Go on to think together about situations in which your youngsters may have to
   do things they don't much want to, (eg at school, helping around the home
   etc) - do they sulk? disobey? get angry...? As appropriate, pray together for the
   grace to follow Joseph's example!

ACTIVITIES:
1. Slave Day!

Ask everyone to get into pairs. Choose a random method to decide who will be
the 'slave' and who will be the 'owner' in each pair. Simply have the 'slaves' do
whatever their 'owners' ask of them. Then swap over! Talk together about the
experience afterwards.

2. 'Prayer Maps'

Help your youngsters draw a map of the places they will be going in the next
week. It might be good to give each youngster a simple outline map of your town
or area to work from! Have your youngsters locate and mark their homes,
schools, your club's venue etc. Give them time to colour the maps and add in
details. Remind your youngsters that God was with Joseph when he was sold as a
slave in Egypt far away from his home... Then pray together, thanking God for
being with us wherever we go this week (and the next...)!

Extra:
If you are using 'Joseph and His Amazing Technicolour Dreamcoat', 'Poor, Poor
Joseph' fits in with this session.

KEY VERSE:
[The Lord says:] "When you pass through the waters, I will be with you..."
                      Isaiah 43:2

Checklist

☐ ....

☐ ....

☐ ....

☐ ....

☐ ....

☐ ....

☐

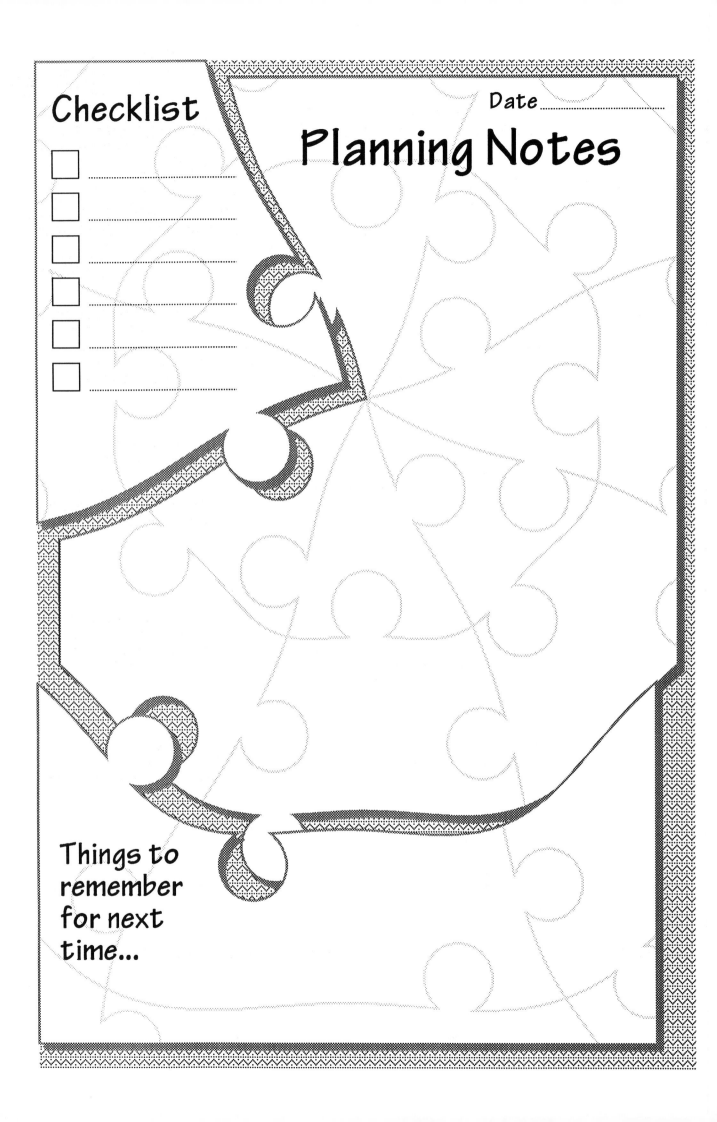

Date _____

Planning Notes

Things to
remember
for next
time...

TITLE: Prisoner

BIBLE BASE: **Genesis 39:6b-40:23** (Joseph is Put into Prison <u>&</u> Joseph Interprets Two Dreams)

WE WANT OUR YOUNGSTERS TO...
- **... know that, even when things get worse, God is always there!**
- **... understand that standing up for what God says is right may be costly... but it is always worth it in the end!**

LEAD-IN: ➤ In advance, think of a situation relevant to your youngsters in which someone tries to persuade someone else to do something wrong. ◄ Work out a short play with other leaders and helpers. Act it out for your youngsters, stopping the action as the central character has to decide what to do... Ask your youngsters for 'advice'. Encourage them to think through each idea with questions like: **what would happen if he/she did this?** Sum up.

HOW TO START:
- ◆ Begin: *Joseph ran as fast as he could. He heard shouting behind him, but he did not stop or look back. What was he going to say to his boss Potiphar...?*
- ◆ Don't get drawn into the details of the story... and don't assume that everyone will see that Joseph did the 'right' thing when he refused to accept Potiphar's wife's offer! Simply highlight the fact that Joseph acted to please God in this situation.

ACTIVITIES:

1. Over to YOU!

Ask your youngsters to get into small groups. Ask each group to make up a short drama about people trying to persuade someone to do something wrong (along the lines of the LEAD-IN). Have an opportunity to see each group's ideas. Use them to help your youngsters talk about the peer-pressure they face in real life. Talk together about realistic, practical solutions. And pray!

2. Like Joseph

➤ In advance, organise something to help your youngsters become aware of and concerned about being in prison. Choose carefully! Possibilities include:
- Having an exciting story of a Christian wrongly imprisoned, perhaps for their faith;
- Presenting the story of Anne Frank;
- Sending for information from a human rights organisation and getting involved as a group as suggested. ◄

Extra: If you are using 'Joseph and His Amazing Technicolour Dreamcoat', 'Close Every Door to Me' fits in with this session.

KEY VERSE: *Happy are those who don't listen to the wicked (...), who don't do what evil people do.* Psalm 1:1

Checklist

☐ ....

☐ ....

☐ ....

☐ ....

☐ ....

☐

Date ....

Planning Notes

Things to remember for next time...

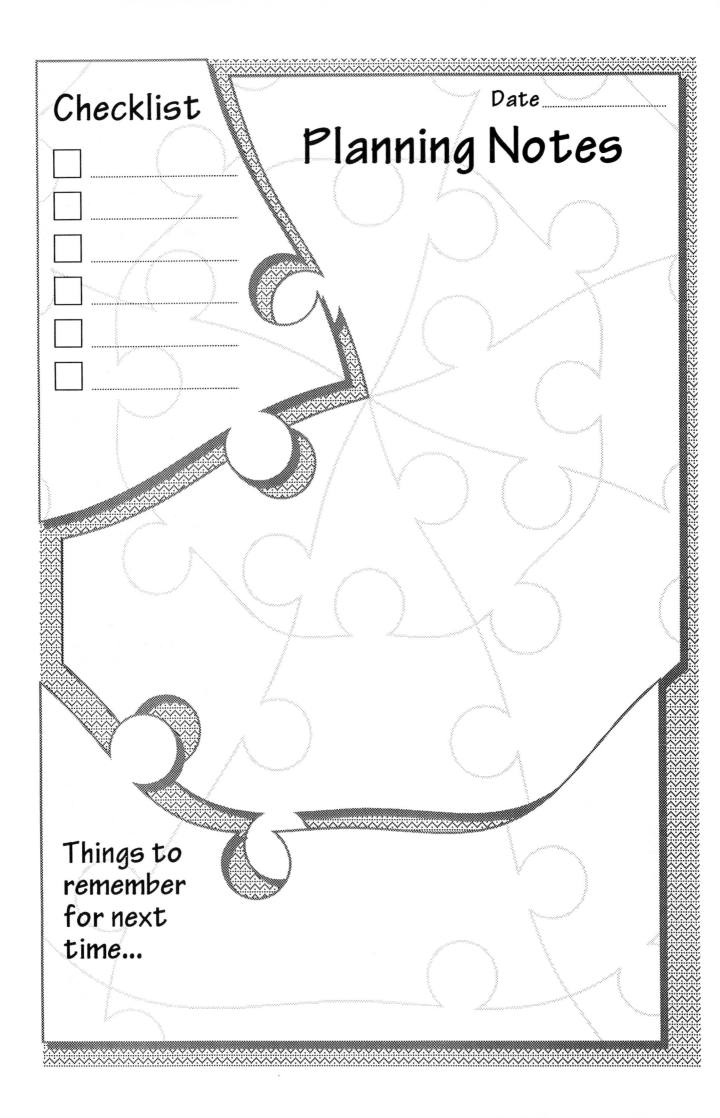

TITLE: Ruler

Joseph
4 of 5

BIBLE BASE: **Genesis 41:1-57** (*from* The King's Dreams *to* Joseph is Made Ruler over Egypt)

WE WANT OUR YOUNGSTERS TO...
... **understand that our all-powerful God works to bring good out of difficult situations;**
... **consider the importance of personal qualities such as wisdom.**

LEAD-IN: Have a famous people quiz! ➤ In advance, get together pictures of about ten well-known people from sport, music, public life etc - make sure they are relevant to your youngsters! Cut out part of each picture, (eg hair, eyes and nose only). Stick each one on a separate piece of paper. Number them all. ◄ Tack them around the walls of your meeting room before anyone arrives. Ask your youngsters to get into pairs. Give each pair a piece of paper and a pencil. Have everyone move round and try to identify the famous people! Then talk together about them and the **qualities** which have helped them do well.

HOW TO START: ◆ Begin: ***Pharaoh woke up with a start. It was the middle of the night. It was completely dark and all he could hear was the sound of his own breathing. Pharaoh felt worried and confused: what a strange dream...!***
◆ Bring out the qualities and abilities Joseph had to be Ruler over Egypt - and how he clearly recognised that they came from God!

ACTIVITIES: **1. What About US?**

➤ In advance, make a list of about ten personal qualities, (eg kind, honest, wise etc), large enough for everyone to see. ◄ Now ask your youngsters to get into pairs. Firstly, ask everyone to draw a portrait of their partner. Then ask everyone to identify the qualities their partner has - they may need help with this! Ask everyone to write these qualities under the portrait they have drawn. Display them all. Use them to encourage individuals and spur them to think about how they can use and develop their qualities. And pray!

2. 'If I Were Prime Minister...'

Have your youngsters get into groups. Now tell them that you are going to have an imaginary election! Ask each group to choose a candidate to run for 'Prime Minister'. Now ask each group to decide together what it would do to make the world a better place to live in. Perhaps have the groups present their ideas on posters <u>or</u> in 'party political broadcasts' <u>or</u> very short 'speeches' made by the candidates! Then have a vote!

Extra: If you are using 'Joseph and His Amazing Technicolour Dreamcoat', 'Pharaoh's Dream' fits in with this session.

KEY VERSE: *God has made us what we are. In Christ Jesus, God made us to do good works...*
Ephesians 2:10

Checklist

- [ ]
- [ ]
- [ ]
- [ ]
- [ ]
- [ ]

Date _____

Planning Notes

Things to
remember
for next
time...

TITLE: Altogether Again!

BIBLE BASE: **Genesis 42:1-46:7** (*from* The Dreams Come True *to* Jacob Goes to Egypt)

WE WANT OUR YOUNGSTERS TO...

... recognise God's hand in this reconciliation;

... trust Him in the difficult situations in which they find themselves.

LEAD-IN:

[Be sensitive and tactful! This could bring up some difficult family situations...]

➤ In advance, ask your youngsters to bring in photos, letters and so on from friends and family who live in other parts of the country or world. ◄ Talk together about the people and this situation, (eg have any of your youngsters visited the person? Would they like to? How do they keep in touch? etc).

HOW TO START:

◆ If at all possible, involve everyone in acting out this final part of the story - you will need people to play JOSEPH, JACOB and THE BROTHERS... everyone else can be servants or donkeys! Establish one part of your meeting room as Egypt and have Canaan as far away as possible! Move between the two 'countries' acting out the events as you tell the story.

◆ Begin: *So Joseph had it all - a beautiful palace, power, money and servants to do everything for him! But sometimes he still felt sad. It had been such a long time since he'd seen his dad, his brothers, his sisters, his home... Joseph often thought about them and wondered what they might be doing...*

◆ Focus on the joy as the whole family is reunited!

ACTIVITIES:

1. The Joseph Story

➤ In advance, make a list of the key incidents in Joseph's life, large enough for everyone to see. ◄ Ask your youngsters to get into pairs or small groups. Either ask each group to choose a part of the story or assign one to them! Now have each group make a picture or model using any materials you are able to provide. As you put all the pictures and/or models together, arrange them on different levels to show the 'up's and down's' in Joseph's life. As appropriate, talk about where God was in Joseph's story, and help your youngsters appreciate where He is in the 'up's and down's' of their own lives.

2. Prayer World

Provide a map of the world or globe. Have your youngsters draw small pictures of the people they talked about in the LEAD-IN or write their names on pieces of paper. As a group, put the pictures or names on the map or globe. Pray that God will take care of these people, just as He took care of Joseph and his family when they were apart. As appropriate, also pray sensitively for the split families in your group.

Extra:

If you are using 'Joseph and His Amazing Technicolour Dreamcoat', 'So Jacob Came to Egypt' fits in with this session.

KEY VERSE:

God turned your evil into good to save the lives of many people... Genesis 50:20

Checklist

- [ ]
- [ ]
- [ ]
- [ ]
- [ ]
- [ ]

Date _____

Planning Notes

Things to remember for next time...

TITLE: A Widow

BIBLE BASE: **Ruth 1:1-22**   (Ruth Stays with Naomi)

WE WANT OUR YOUNGSTERS TO...

... know that God never stops caring for people, (although sometimes it might look as if He has!)

... consider how they can be loyal, like Ruth was;

LEAD-IN: ➤ In advance, look at the Bible passage and carefully divide today's part of the story into about six parts, (eg 'Naomi, her husband and two sons leave Bethlehem because there is a food shortage'; 'Naomi is sad because her husband has died' etc). ◄ Ask your youngsters to get into pairs <u>or</u> small groups. Give each group a large piece of paper and some coloured pencils <u>or</u> pens. Now give each group one of the story parts and ask them to do a large drawing to go with it...

HOW TO START: ◆ ...Have each group show its picture as you tell the story!
◆ Begin: ***"Poor Naomi!" thought Ruth to herself. As she looked back, it seemed that Naomi's life had been one tragedy after another! First there was the famine, which drove her whole family from their home in Bethlehem...***
◆ Help your youngsters think about how Naomi and Ruth might have felt about God in their situation, (eg 'has He forgotten about us?')...
◆ ...State clearly that God never stops caring for us... (Your youngsters will have to wait and see how He cared for Naomi and Ruth!)
◆ Keep the pictures on display as a 'comic strip' - perhaps add a 'to be continued' sign at the end!

ACTIVITIES: **1. This is <u>My</u> Life!**

Give each youngster a piece of paper and some coloured pencils <u>or</u> pens. Ask everyone to draw a comic strip of their lives so far in about six pictures - you may well need to help younger children think about what to include in this! Now ask them to show and tell their stories to one or two close friends <u>and/or</u> leaders. Help them see how God has been caring for them - whether they have been aware of it or not! As appropriate to your youngsters and their situations, state that God cares now and always will. And thank Him!

2. Stick!

Think of a quiz with forfeits <u>or</u> any game in which someone can be OUT <u>or</u> 'tagged'. This time, ask your youngsters to get into pairs. Each pair decides on one 'player' to actually do the quiz <u>or</u> game... his/her partner 'sticks' to him/her throughout. Any forfeit happens to **both** youngsters in a pair! Ask the 'players' and 'stickers' how they felt. Use this experience to help your youngsters explore what it means to 'stick' with someone through thick and thin like Ruth did! Then pray!

KEY VERSE: *Depend on the Lord; trust him and he will take care of you.* Psalm 37:5

Checklist

☐ ....
☐ ....
☐ ....
☐ ....
☐ ....
☐ ....

Date _____

Planning Notes

Things to remember for next time...

TITLE: A Worker

BIBLE BASE: **Ruth 2:1-23** (Ruth Meets Boaz)

WE WANT OUR YOUNGSTERS TO...

> ... **see that God cares and provides for people;**
> ... **look for 'evidence' of His provision for their needs - and thank Him.**

LEAD-IN: Spread some rice out onto a large tray - if possible, mix it with something else, such as sand <u>or</u> grass cuttings. Ask your youngsters to get into teams of about six. Station the teams around your meeting room. Place the tray in the middle, at the same distance from each team. When you say 'go', one person from each team runs to the tray, gets one grain of rice and runs back to his/her team. The second person then goes ...and so on. Allow about three minutes for this. Then see which team has collected the most rice. Ask: **would you like to collect your food like this every day?**

HOW TO START:
◆ Begin: *Ruth's back was aching from bending down for so long. And it was so hot! She seemed to have been in the field for hours, moving the stalks and stony soil around with her hands to find any ears of grain the harvesters had left behind. But as she looked in her basket, there hardly seemed to be enough grain to feed a bird, let alone Naomi and herself...*
◆ Bring out clearly how God was 'behind the scenes', making sure that Ruth and Naomi had enough to eat...
◆ To continue the 'comic strip' from last session, perhaps have your youngsters get into groups and produce a drawing for part of today's story.

ACTIVITIES: **1. Thank You!**

Linking in with how God cared and provided for Ruth and Naomi, 'brainstorm' the things God provides for us - you may find that your youngsters have to think quite hard about this as they may take lots of things for granted! Now ask your youngsters to work out a rap <u>or</u> rhyme <u>or</u> song <u>or</u> poem <u>or</u>... to thank God for these things. Have an opportunity to hear everyone's ideas.

2. Edible Pictures

Give each youngster a paper plate <u>or</u> round piece of paper. <u>Either</u> ask your youngsters to think of their favourite meal and have them 'make' it on the plate using coloured paper, card, wool, scraps of cloth etc, and glue to stick it all down! <u>Alternatively</u>, have a selection of edible things such as pasta, beans and pulses <u>or</u> fresh salad ingredients, and ask your youngsters to use them to create a picture.

KEY VERSE: *Give thanks to the Lord, because he is good. (...) He gives food to every living creature.* Psalm 136:1 & 25

Checklist

☐ ....

☐ ....

☐ ....

☐ ....

☐ ....

☐ ....

Planning Notes

Things to
remember
for next
time...

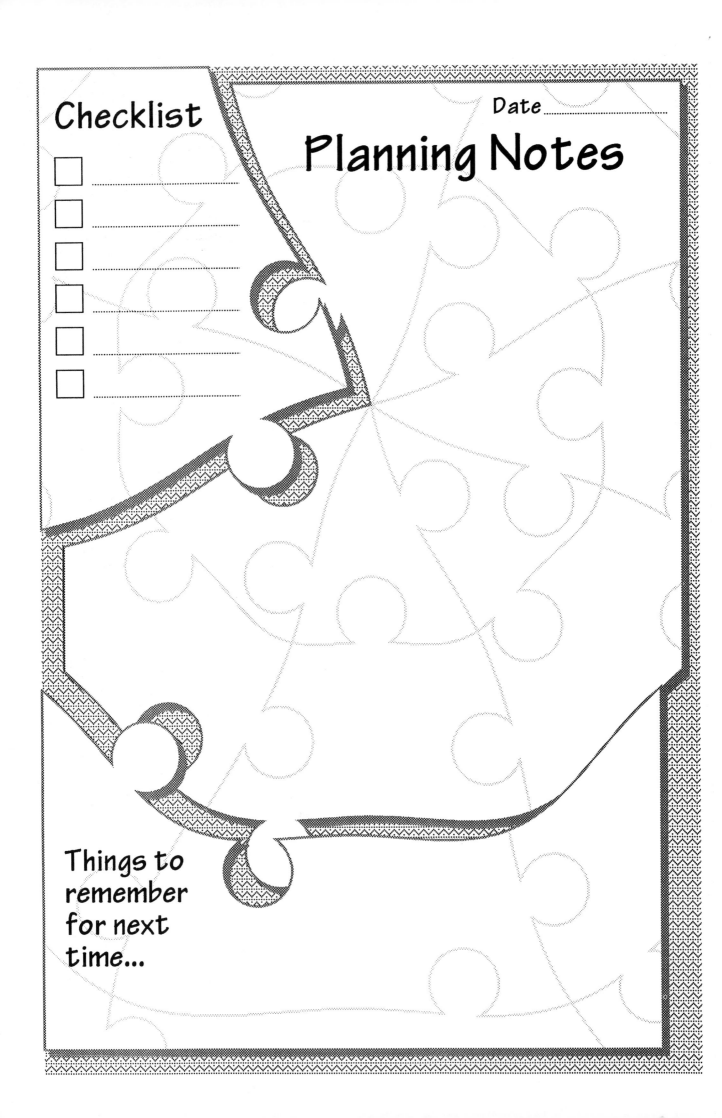

TITLE: A Wife

BIBLE BASE: **Ruth 3:1-4:22** (Naomi's Plan <u>&</u> Boaz
Marries Ruth)

WE WANT OUR YOUNGSTERS TO...
... **know that God cares about people's
relationships - including marriage!**
... **thank Him and pray for the special
relationships in their lives.**

LEAD-IN: Give your youngsters one minute to think of all
the people they know! <u>Either</u> ask them to find a
partner, have one person talk and then swap over; <u>Or</u> have everyone write names
down! Talk together about the different kinds of relationships we have,
(eg friends, parents, brothers/sisters, teachers etc). Ask: **which of these people
are most special to you?** Perhaps have a photo of your best friends and family to
show. Talk together about what makes these people special to us. Bring out the
idea that relationships of all kinds are really precious!

HOW TO START: ◆ Begin: *Ruth listened carefully as Naomi explained what she should do: "Go
and wash yourself. Put on some perfume... and your best clothes! Then
go down to where Boaz is preparing some of his grain. But wait until it
gets dark...!"*
◆ Talk about God's part in this 'happy ending'! If appropriate, also let your
youngsters know that Ruth and Boaz were the ancestors of some very special
people (*Matthew 1:5, 6 & 16*)!
◆ To continue the 'comic strip' from last session, perhaps have your youngsters
get into groups and produce a drawing for the final parts of the story.

ACTIVITIES: **1. Family and Friends Circle**

Give each youngster two circles (A and B) cut from stiff paper <u>or</u> card. Everyone
divides both circles into six sections. Ask your youngsters to draw a picture <u>or</u>
write the name of one person who is special to them in each of the six sections
on circle A. They then cut one section out of circle B. Ask them to put the circles
together - B on top of A - and put a split pin through the centre. A different
person appear as the circles are moved around! As appropriate, use these to help
your youngsters thank God and pray for the people and relationships on them.

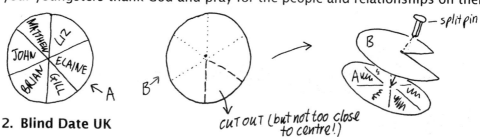

2. Blind Date UK

With older youngsters, have a low-key version of the TV programme 'Blind Date'!
Have your youngsters get into small groups to make up a person, (eg interests,
ambitions, job etc) and write this information down on separate pieces of paper;
<u>Alternatively</u>, do this yourself in advance! Stage it as close to the TV show as you
can! <u>Either</u> have three self-confident volunteers choosing a piece of paper and
playing the person on it <u>or</u> just read three out for a 'contestant' to choose from.
Have several rounds, as appropriate. You may well have some interesting
conversations as a result of this...!

KEY VERSE: *You are my Lord. Every good thing I have comes from you. Psalm 16:2*

Checklist

- [ ]
- [ ]
- [ ]
- [ ]
- [ ]
- [ ]

Date _____

Planning Notes

Things to remember for next time...

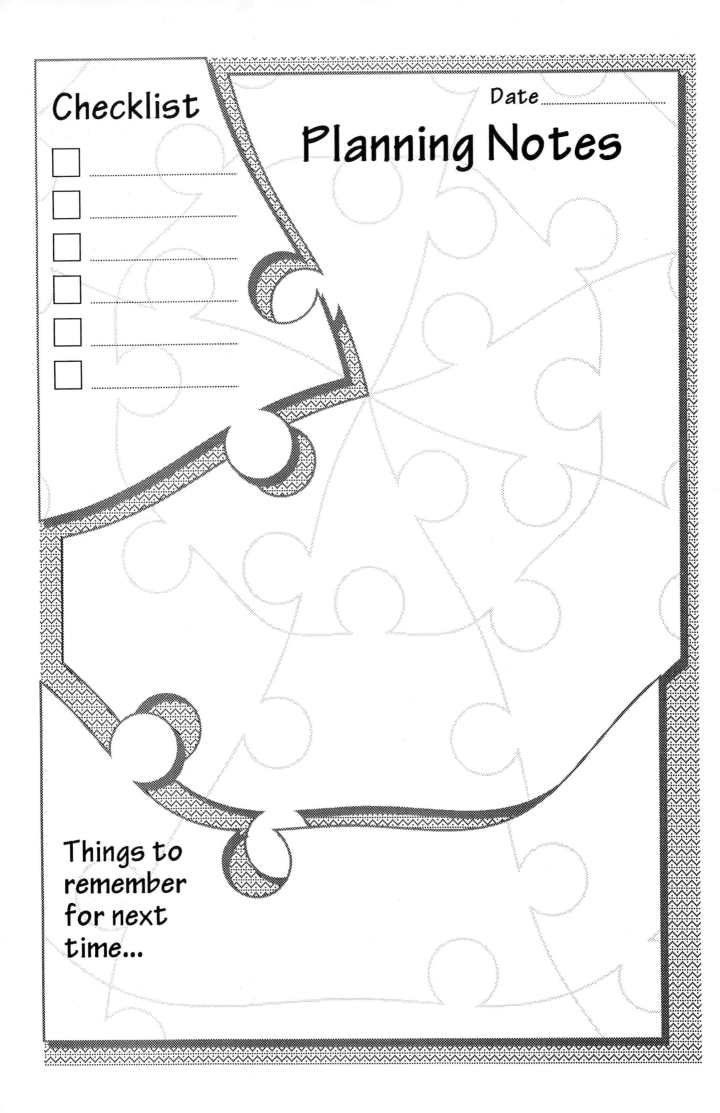

TITLE: **One Special Baby**

BIBLE BASE: Matthew 1:18-25 (The Birth of Jesus Christ) **& Luke 1:30-35** (An Angel Appears to Mary)

WE WANT OUR YOUNGSTERS TO...
... see why Jesus was unique, even before He was born!
... know that He came to rescue us.

LEAD-IN: Ask: **what do you think of when I say CHRISTMAS?** Now ask your youngsters to make a collage of images and words about Christmas, using any materials you can provide, (eg coloured pens, pencils, old Christmas cards, bits of decoration etc). They could do this individually <u>or</u> in groups <u>or</u> altogether. Talk together about the collages... but don't question where Jesus is (or is not!) at this point!

HOW TO START: ◆ ➤ In advance, look through the Bible texts and list each of the things the angel told Mary and Joseph about Jesus before He was born, (eg His name, who He is, what He came to do etc). As appropriate to your youngsters, draw a symbol <u>and/or</u> write a few simple words for each one on separate pieces of paper. ◄ Use them to focus attention during **and** after the story!
    ◆ Begin: *When you were growing in your mum's body, people were already talking about you! People were wondering what you were going to look like, what you would grow up to be... But it was all guess-work: nobody <u>really</u> knew what you were going to be like. It was different with Jesus...*

ACTIVITIES:

1. Who? Where? Why?

➤ In advance, think of four 'who-where-why's', (eg DOCTOR-HOSPITAL-TO MAKE PEOPLE BETTER.) Add JESUS-EARTH-TO RESCUE US. Write each part of each one on separate pieces of paper - large enough for everyone to see! Add simple drawings, as appropriate. ◄ Spread all 15 pieces of paper out on a table, face down. Youngsters take it in turns to turn over three of them - if they make a 'who-where-why', the youngster keeps them; if not, he/she turns them over again! Continue until all the 'who-where-why's' have been found!

2. Angel Decoration

[You may need to make some templates for this in advance!]

Have your youngsters cut a semi-circle from white paper <u>or</u> card and bend it round to make a cone. Stick the cone together with glue <u>or</u> sticky tape. Then have them cut out and colour wing shapes, a trumpet, a head and arms. Stick these to the cone shape. You can, of course, develop this basic idea with other materials, (eg coloured paper, silver foil etc). Finally, hang the angel up with a length of sewing cotton <u>or</u> string <u>or</u> wool.

Extra: You could organise a Christmas event such as a Nativity Play <u>or</u> visual/musical presentation to be performed at the end of this series! Plan and practise something relevant to your youngsters based on this part of the Christmas Story.

KEY VERSE: *[The angel said:] "...you will name him Jesus, because he will save his people from their sins."* Matthew 1:21

Checklist

☐ ....
☐ ....
☐ ....
☐ ....
☐ ....
☐ ....

Date ....

Planning Notes

Things to
remember
for next
time...

TITLE: Two Travellers

BIBLE BASE: Luke 2:1-7 (The Birth of Jesus)

WE WANT OUR YOUNGSTERS TO...
- ... see that Jesus was born into a difficult and uncomfortable situation;
- ... think about how to keep going...

LEAD-IN: Ask everyone to think of a journey they particularly remember. Either altogether or in small groups, invite individuals to say a little about the journey, (eg where they went, how they travelled, what it was like (long, exciting, tiring) etc). Then think together about what you need for a journey -perhaps bring in a large bag or suitcase and decide what should go into it!

HOW TO START:
- ◆ ➤ Mary and Joseph travelled about 70 miles (110 kms)... In advance, work out what an equivalent journey would be in your own area and/or get a map to show the journey from Nazareth to Bethlehem. ◄
- ◆ Tell the story from Mary and/or Joseph's point of view. ➤ Perhaps make and write imaginary postcards or short letters from Mary and Joseph in advance. Put them around your meeting room. ◄ 'Travel round' as a group, reading out and talking about the 'postcards' as you go.
- ◆ Concentrate on helping your youngsters see how difficult it would have been for both Mary and Joseph to keep going.
- ◆ Talk together about times when we find it hard to keep going...
- ◆ ...Then, as appropriate, talk about the difference it makes knowing God is always there for us and about how He can help us keep going when we feel like giving up. And pray!

ACTIVITIES:

1. Census

➤ In advance, make up simple census forms - use words and/or symbols, as appropriate. Include name, address, date of birth, pets... be sensitive about any other information you ask for! ◄ Give each youngster several copies of the form. Use them to conduct a mock census in your group!

2. Travel Game

Ask your youngsters to get into small groups. Have each group make and play a simple board game based on Joseph and Mary's journey from Nazareth to Bethlehem! Alternatively, make it yourself in advance! Have dice and counters to move round a simple circuit with marked squares, such as 'the donkey needs to be fed - miss a go!'

Extra: Plan and practise the second part of your Christmas event!

KEY VERSE: *...our Lord Jesus Christ was kind enough to give up all his riches and become poor, so that you could become rich.* 2 Corinthians 8:9 (CEV)

Checklist

☐ ....

☐ ....

☐ ....

☐ ....

☐ ....

☐ ....

Date _____

Planning Notes

Things to remember for next time...

TITLE: Three Special Gifts

BIBLE BASE: Matthew 2:1-12 (Wise Men Come to Visit Jesus)

WE WANT OUR YOUNGSTERS TO...

... **understand that the three gifts foretold important things about Jesus and His life.**

LEAD-IN:
[Look after these things carefully and ensure that they get home again safely!]

➤ In advance, ask everyone to bring in <u>or</u> think about a special gift. If possible, also bring something given to a baby. ◄ In small groups, ask everyone to show <u>and/or</u> talk about the gift. Gently correct the idea that special equals expensive! Also, guard against youngsters trying to get 'one up' on each other!

HOW TO START:

◆ ➤ In advance, find things to represent the three gifts: GOLD (gold coloured metal <u>or</u> paper), FRANKINCENSE (incense sticks) and MYRRH (scented hair <u>or</u> body cream). Wrap each of the gifts. ◄

◆ Ask: **what presents would you give to a baby?** Link in with the LEAD-IN, as appropriate.

◆ As you tell the story, have a youngster unwrap a gift at a time. Explain its significance in simple terms: GOLD for a king, FRANKINCENSE for God, MYRRH for burial...

◆ Begin: ***When some wise men came to visit Jesus, they brought three unusual gifts with them...***

◆ Perhaps take this opportunity to give each youngster a small gift - ➤ wrap them and attach name labels in advance! ◄

ACTIVITIES:

1. What Can I Give?

Ask your youngsters to get into small teams. Give each team some newspaper and string <u>and/or</u> sticky tape. Now ask each team to 'giftwrap' one of its members! Have a time limit for this. Look at each team's 'gift' and decide which has been wrapped the best. Use this as a 'springboard' to talk simply about giving ourselves to Jesus, as appropriate.

2. Give a Gift

Have your youngsters make a simple Christmas gift to give to someone, (eg some no-cook sweets, decorated biscuits, a calendar, card, simple toy <u>or</u> game...)

Extra: Plan and practise the third part of your Christmas event!

KEY VERSE: *[Jesus said:] "Give, and you will receive."* Luke 6:38a

Checklist

☐ ....
☐ ....
☐ ....
☐ ....
☐ ....
☐ ....

Date ....

Planning Notes

Things to
remember
for next
time...

TITLE: Escape!

BIBLE BASE: Matthew 2:12-23 (*from* Jesus'
Parents Take Him to Egypt *to* Joseph
and Mary Return)

WE WANT OUR YOUNGSTERS TO...

- ... recognise that God warned Mary and Joseph about the danger;
- ... see that God kept Jesus safe from harm;
- ... know that we can ask for God's help and protection.

LEAD-IN:

[Be sensitive! This could be real to some youngsters...]

Give everyone a piece of paper and a pen <u>or</u> pencil. Then set the scene: ask your youngsters to imagine that they have to escape tonight and that it's impossible to know when they'll be back again... Ask them to write <u>or</u> draw on their piece of paper a list of what they want to take with them. Allow only one minute for this! Then say that the youngsters must cross off anything that would not fit in a small suitcase... Get together in small groups and talk about your youngsters' lists - did they think of essential things like food?! Ask: **how did you feel about having to make such choices?**

HOW TO START:

- ◆ Begin: *No time to lose! Mary and Joseph ran around the house, grabbing the things they would need for the journey. They had no choice: God had told Joseph in a dream that they would have to leave tonight, or Jesus would be in grave danger...*
- ◆ As appropriate, help your youngsters think of things which present a danger to them - but be careful not to generate an atmosphere of fear! Talk about how God protects us... then pray!

ACTIVITIES:

[If you do not have hiding places around your meeting room, play a game which involves a 'safe place' instead!]

1. 'A Hiding Place'

Have a simple hiding game of some kind, such as 'Hide and Hunt'! Have your youngsters get into two teams - A and B. Establish one area as a base. Team A stays at the base for 30 seconds, whilst team B members go off to hide. Time team A to see how long it takes them to find everyone from team B and bring them back to base! Then swap round. The team which does this in the shortest time, wins! Focus on hiding in this game: use it to help your youngsters appreciate the 'picture' of God in the KEY VERSE.

2. Like Joseph, Mary and Jesus

➤ In advance, organise something to help your youngsters become aware of and concerned about refugees today. You may, of course, have people in your group with first-hand experience of this. Possibilities include:
- Having a speaker;
- Sending for some information (preferably slides <u>or</u> video <u>or</u> large posters) from a charity and getting involved as suggested. ◄

Extra:

Plan and practise the fourth and final part of your Christmas event!

KEY VERSE:

You are my hiding place. Psalm 32:7

Checklist

- ☐ ....
- ☐ ....
- ☐ ....
- ☐ ....
- ☐ ....
- ☐ ....

Date ....

Planning Notes

Things to
remember
for next
time...

TITLE: The Lost Sheep

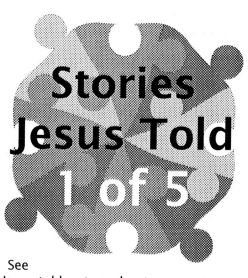

BIBLE BASE: Luke 15:4-7 (The Lost Sheep)

WE WANT OUR YOUNGSTERS TO...

... understand how Jesus is like a Good Shepherd;

... understand how we are like lost sheep!

LEAD-IN:

➤ In advance, cut 20 sheep shapes out of paper <u>or</u> card. ◄ Hide them around your meeting room before your youngsters arrive. Send everyone to search for the 20 lost sheep. See who can find the most. Lead in by saying that Jesus told a story about a shepherd who looked for **one** lost sheep...

HOW TO START:

◆ ➤ In advance, write the following out large on separate pieces of paper: 'KNOWS EACH ONE', 'CARES', 'LOVES', 'PUTS HIMSELF IN DANGER' 'THE GOOD SHEPHERD' and 'JESUS'. Also, find some pictures of sheep to show. ◄

◆ Put up the heading 'THE GOOD SHEPHERD': add the other words as you tell the story...

◆ Begin: *What would you do all day if you were a sheep - eat most of the time?! You would probably be very happy as long as you were with other sheep and had a good shepherd to look after you... Now imagine that one day you wander off and suddenly find yourself alone and lost. Imagine that there are thieves in the area who steal sheep, and wolves who attack them! How would you feel? What would you most want? This is what happened to a sheep in a story Jesus told...*

◆ ... Add 'JESUS' before 'THE GOOD SHEPHERD' as you explain that Jesus was really talking about Him and us!

ACTIVITIES:

[You may need to make some templates for this in advance!]

1. Fluffy Sheep

Ask your youngsters to cut a sheep shape out of card. Now have them stick cotton wool on it and colour it in. On the other side, <u>either</u> have them write the KEY VERSE, <u>or</u> some information about your club, so that they can give the sheep to a friend as an invitation!

2. Sheepfold Game

[If you have younger children, let them shout instructions as well as blowing the whistle!]

Set up a 'sheepfold' using chairs and string. Ask your youngsters to get into teams of about four. Ask each team to decide on one person to be a 'shepherd' - the rest are 'sheep'! Explain that the 'shepherd' will need to guide his/her **blindfolded** 'sheep' into the 'sheepfold' by blowing a whistle - no talking allowed! Then give the teams time to decide on a code, (eg two blows means turn left etc). Choose a team to go first. Blindfold the 'sheep' - and run the game! Time each team: the quickest wins!

KEY VERSE: *[Jesus said:] "I am the good shepherd."* John 10:14

Checklist

- ☐ ....
- ☐ ....
- ☐ ....
- ☐ ....
- ☐ ....
- ☐ ....

Date _____

Planning Notes

Things to remember for next time...

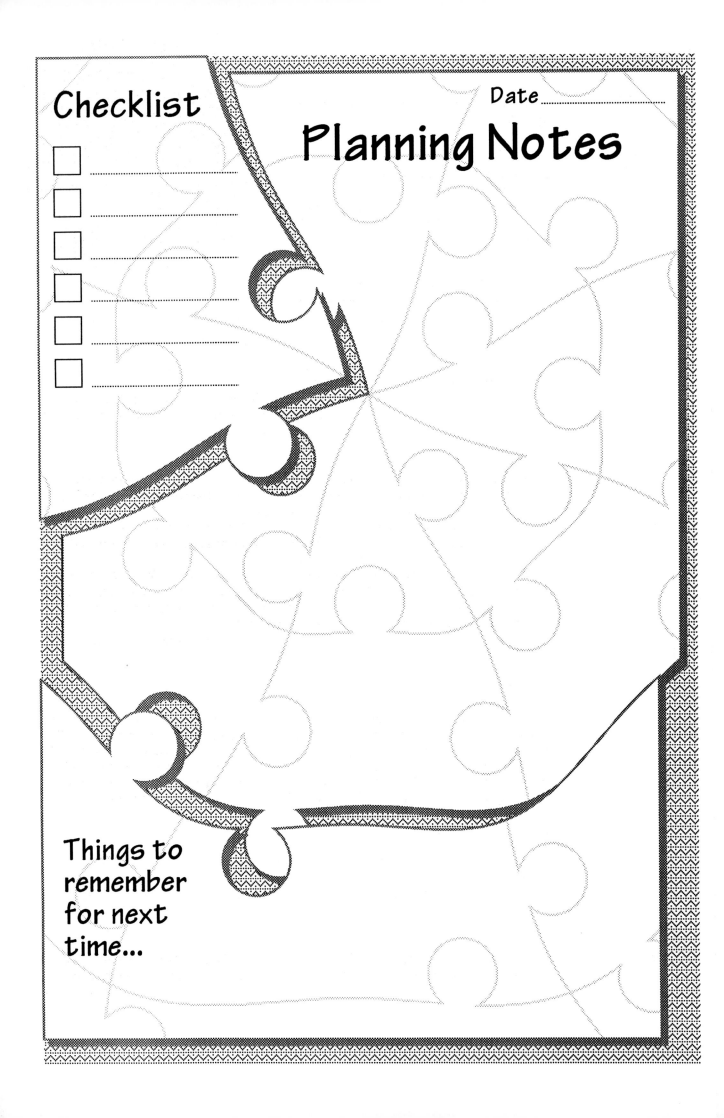

TITLE: The Sower

BIBLE BASE: **Matthew 13:1-23** (The Parable of
the Sower)

WE WANT OUR YOUNGSTERS TO...
- ... **learn that we can listen to God in many ways;**
- ... **realise that, when we hear something about God, we have a choice about what we do with it!**

LEAD-IN: Have everyone in a circle. Whisper the first message
below **once** to the youngster on your left, who then whispers it **once** to the youngster on his/her left... and so on. The last person says out loud what he/she thinks the message is. Correct any mistakes! Do the same with the second message:

1. *'Once there was a man who went out to sow corn'* (v 3b)
2. *'...they listen, but do not hear or understand'* (v 13b)

Talk together about this: Did your youngsters listen to the message? Did they hear it? Did they understand it? Use this to bring out, very simply, the difference between 'listening', 'hearing' and 'understanding'.

HOW TO START:
- ◆ ➤ In advance, find some wheat to show - <u>either</u> a picture <u>or</u> the real thing! Also, prepare cues by writing <u>and/or</u> drawing what happened to the seed in each of the soils on a separate piece of paper. ◄
- ◆ Ask your youngsters to get into four groups. Give each group one of the cues. <u>Either</u> ask each group to prepare a large picture <u>or</u> act out what happened to the seed in their soil! Include these as you tell the story.
- ◆ Begin: ***Many, many people came to hear Jesus that day. When He started to speak, everybody in the crowd was quiet so that they could listen - a nice story about a farmer? Well, that's what they heard, but who really understood what Jesus was trying to tell them...?***
- ◆ As appropriate, challenge your youngsters about which soil is most like them.

ACTIVITIES: **1. How do I listen?**

Have a portable radio hidden in a bag. Tell everyone to be very quiet because you can hear talking and singing. Say things like: "Can you hear, that's a choir?!" Be surprised that no-one else can hear it. Then turn the hidden radio on and tune in to different programmes: the singing and voices were there all the time - we just needed help to listen! Lead into a brief discussion/explanation of how we can listen to God - be absolutely clear about this and sort out any confusions!

2. To Listen or Not to Listen?

Ask your youngsters to get into small groups. Ask each group to make up a short drama about what happens when someone does not really listen - it could be funny <u>or</u> serious! Have an opportunity to see and talk about each group's drama.

KEY VERSE: *[Jesus said:] "...the seed that fell on the good ground (...) is like the person who hears the teaching and understands it. That person grows and produces fruit..."*
                                                                Matthew 13:23

Checklist

☐ ....
☐ ....
☐ ....
☐ ....
☐ ....
☐ ....

Date ....

Planning Notes

Things to
remember
for next
time...

TITLE: The Unforgiving Servant

BIBLE BASE: Matthew 18: 21-35 (The Parable of the Unforgiving Servant)

WE WANT OUR YOUNGSTERS TO...

... understand that God loves us very much, but He hates the wrong things we do;

... know that God forgives and forgets if we are truly sorry:

... learn that God wants us to be forgiving to others as He is to us.

LEAD-IN:

➤ In advance, write out a few tongue-twisters. Also, write 'SORRY' and 'IT'S ALRIGHT - I FORGIVE YOU' out large on separate pieces of paper. ◄ Have a (non-serious) competition to see who can say the tongue-twisters fastest without making any mistakes! Lead into the story with the comment that there are some things which are harder to say than any of these! Show the two pieces of paper with 'SORRY' and 'IT'S ALRIGHT - I FORGIVE YOU' written on them. Talk briefly about why these things are so hard to say...

HOW TO START:

◆ Ask your youngsters to get into groups of about six. Each group needs a KING and the two SERVANTS - everyone else can be SOLDIERS and GUARDS. Have each group mime the action as you tell the story.

◆ Begin: *The servant was shaking: he knew <u>exactly</u> why the king wanted to see him...*

◆ <u>Either</u> altogether <u>or</u> in small groups, talk together about the three characters in Jesus' story. Ask questions like: **what do you think about what the KING/ SERVANT did? What do you think Jesus is trying to show us in the story?**

ACTIVITIES:

1. Discussion

➤ In advance, think of up to ten situations which might happen to your youngsters, (eg being bullied at school, having their bike stolen etc). Perhaps write each situation out large on poster-sized paper. ◄ <u>Either</u> in small groups <u>or</u> altogether, ask your youngsters to talk about which is hardest to forgive, and why. As appropriate, develop this by asking your youngsters to talk about real experiences in which they have found it hard to forgive someone. Pray together - but be aware that some youngsters may have been deeply hurt by someone, and statements about **having** to forgive may do more harm than good!

2. Design a Banknote

Have your youngsters design their own banknote! Show some real ones first to help them with ideas. Encourage your youngsters to keep their banknotes in their pockets as a reminder to think of:
- people they need to forgive... and then do so;
- things they have done to hurt God and others... and then say 'sorry'!

(<u>Alternatively</u>, if you have some spare foreign coins at home, you could give one to each of your youngsters to keep...)

KEY VERSE:

[Jesus said:] "...if you forgive others for their sins, your Father in heaven will also forgive you for your sins." Matthew 6:14

Checklist

- [ ]
- [ ]
- [ ]
- [ ]
- [ ]
- [ ]

Date _____

Planning Notes

Things to
remember
for next
time...

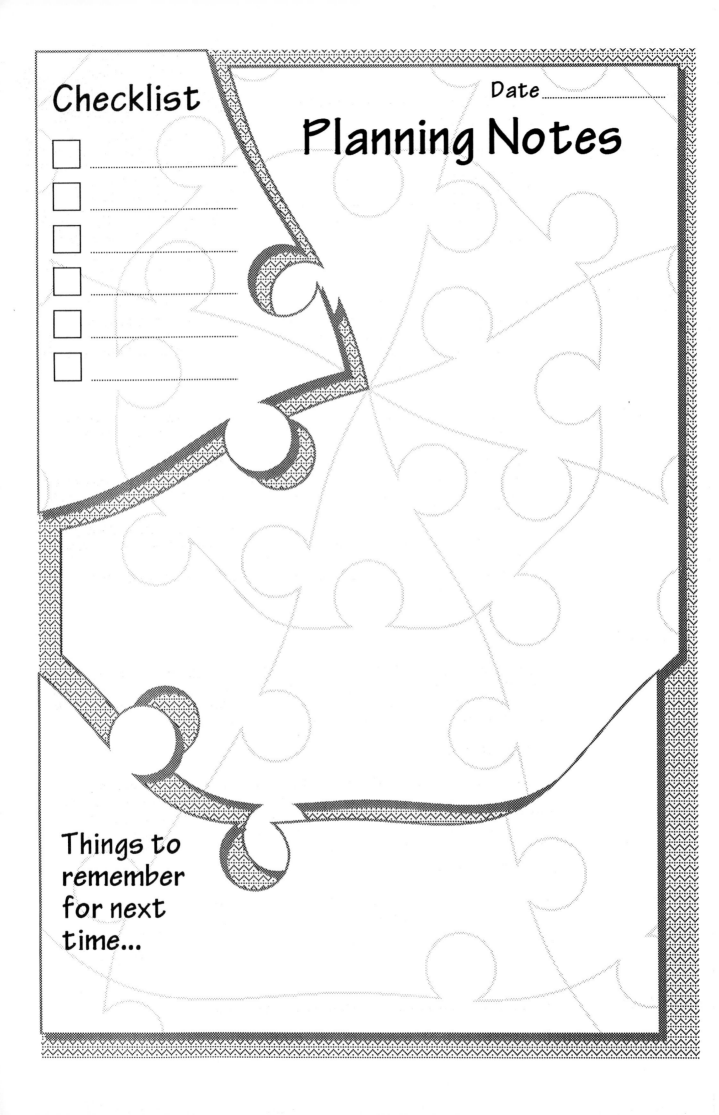

TITLE: The Good Samaritan

BIBLE BASE: Luke 10:25-37   (The Parable of the Good Samaritan)

WE WANT OUR YOUNGSTERS TO...

- ... **understand that there are different kinds of love;**
- ... **see that Jesus is asking us to show love and care in practical ways to people we might not normally care about!**

LEAD-IN:

➤ In advance, record the theme tune of 'Neighbours' onto cassette <u>or</u> make a short video clip from a recent episode. Also, watch at least one episode yourself (if you don't already do so!), so that you know what is going on! Play the tune <u>or</u> the clip and talk about the programme. Ask: **who do you think is being a 'good neighbour' in the programme? And who is not?**

HOW TO START:

◆ You may wish to read the parable from the Bible with other leaders reading <u>and/or</u> acting the parts. <u>Alternatively</u>, update the story using two people from different backgrounds: if you do so, make sure that your youngsters understand the full impact of what Jesus was teaching here!

◆ Begin: *God's ideas about things are often different from ours. Jesus told us to <u>love</u> our neighbours, but did He mean that we should <u>love</u> the people who live next door...?*

◆ Ask your youngsters to think carefully about this - ask: **is there anyone you could show this kind of practical, caring love to, (eg a new pupil in your class, someone who is unpopular at school etc)?**

◆ As appropriate, encourage your youngsters to decide on one thing they could do, then pray about it - and do it!

ACTIVITIES:

1. Drama

Ask your youngsters to think of kinds of people they would not like to touch. Now ask them to get into groups and act out the story again, using one of these examples. Make sure that they do not choose an individual in your group! Have an opportunity to see all these new versions of the parable!

2. Heart Badges

Have your youngsters cut heart shapes from card and then colour them <u>or</u> decorate them with any material you can provide, (eg scraps of material, coloured papers, scrunched-up tissue paper, paper doilies etc). Attach a safety pin to the back of each one with sticky tape, so that it can be worn as a badge. Encourage your youngsters to wear it as a reminder to try and love their neighbours!

BACK

KEY VERSE: *[Jesus said:] "Then go and do what he did."*   Luke 10:37

Checklist

☐ ....
☐ ....
☐ ....
☐ ....
☐ ....
☐ ....

Date ....

Planning Notes

Things to
remember
for next
time...

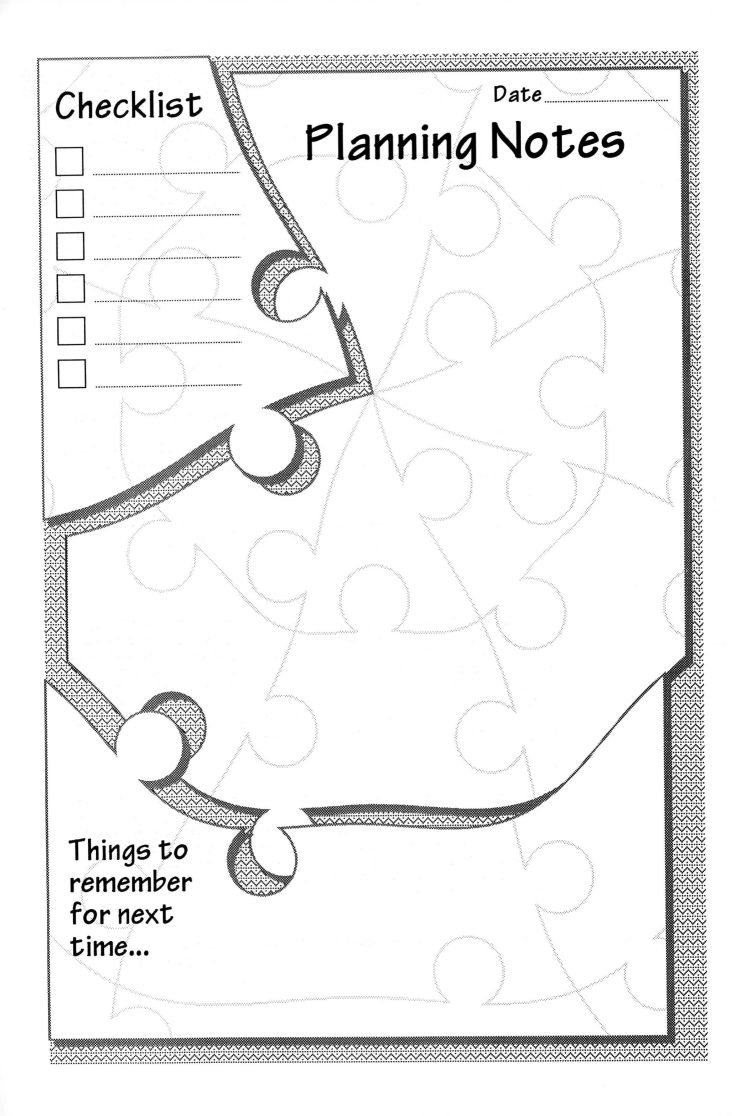

TITLE: **The Two Sons and a Day's Work**

BIBLE BASE: Matthew 21:28-32 (The Parable of the Two Sons)

WE WANT OUR YOUNGSTERS TO...
       ... understand that Jesus asks us to do what we say we will do.

LEAD-IN: ➤ In advance, use your imagination to think of five things you are willing to commit yourself to doing, (eg turning up to the club next week, organising a special event sometime etc). Add a few things which you have no intention of doing, but don't make them too obvious! ◄ For each one, ask your youngsters to decide whether you are going to do it or not - you could take a vote on it! Talk together about how easy it is to promise things and not get round to doing them!

HOW TO START: ◆ ➤ In advance, organise three youngsters <u>and/or</u> leaders to act out a short drama based on the parable. Use the following outline:
       PARENT: You two, come here please. I'd like you to dig the garden today.
       A: Of course... I'd be delighted! (goes off and does something else)
       B: No way - it's not my job to dig the garden! (later changes his/her mind and digs the garden!) ◄
       ◆ Recap on the actions of A and B. Then ask: **who do you think was right?**
       ◆ Help your youngsters think about times when they have been like A... As appropriate to your youngsters, link this with their response to God.

ACTIVITIES: 1. **Consequences**

Ask your youngsters for examples of things they might say they will do, (eg tidy their room, keep out of trouble at school etc). Choose to focus on promises we make to God <u>or</u> to other people, as appropriate to your youngsters. Note these down on a board <u>or</u> poster-sized paper as you go along. Now ask your youngsters to get into small groups. Give each group one of the 'promises'. Ask the groups to 'brainstorm' what might happen if the 'promise' is broken. Have one person from each group report back to everyone else. Use this to highlight the importance of doing what you say you'll do!

2. **Yes and No Game**

Give everyone ten small objects each, (eg beans, dried peas, seeds etc). Have everyone walk round the room asking other people questions, (eg 'have you got brown eyes?' 'is your name ...?' etc). The person questioned **must** answer, but if he/she says 'yes' or 'no', he/she has to give one bean to the questioner. See who has the most beans at the end! Point out that the key to success in this game was being very careful about what you said. Make a link with the teaching content, as appropriate.

KEY VERSE: *[Jesus said:] " Say only yes if you mean yes, and no if you mean no."*
                                                                                Matthew 5:37

Checklist

☐ ....
☐ ....
☐ ....
☐ ....
☐ ....
☐ ....

Date ....

Planning Notes

Things to remember for next time...

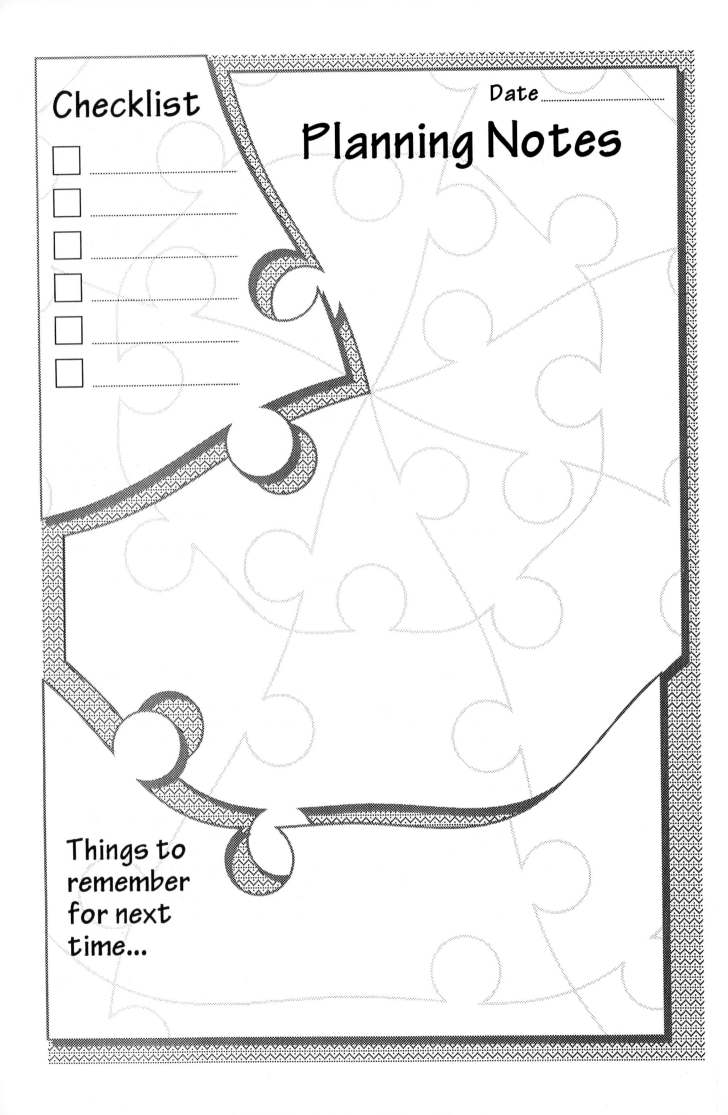

TITLE: ...With Music

BIBLE BASE: **Psalm 150** (Praise the Lord with Music)

WE WANT OUR YOUNGSTERS TO...

... know that the Bible has songs and poems which express people's thoughts and feelings towards God;

... understand that God likes us to use music and poetry to praise Him!

LEAD-IN: ➤ In advance, announce that you are going to have a 'Concert'! ◄ Get as many youngsters and leaders as possible to contribute: they could tell a joke <u>or</u> sing <u>or</u> play a musical instrument <u>or</u> bring their favourite tape to play <u>or</u> read their favourite poem <u>or</u> story... To avoid boredom and showing off, insist that all contributions are kept short!

HOW TO START: ◆ ➤ If appropriate, write out the Psalm on OHP <u>or</u> poster-sized paper in advance, so that everyone will be able to see it! ◄
◆ End the concert by reading (and showing) *Psalm 150*.
◆ Talk about it with questions such as: **what do you think of this poem? What does praise mean? What does the poet want to praise God for? How does he say people should praise God? Who does he say should praise God?**
◆ Go on to introduce this mini-series by:
• explaining that there are quite a lot of poems in the Bible - especially in the Book of Psalms;
• saying that some of the Psalms are happy poems and some are for when we are feeling angry or sad;
• perhaps having your youngsters look in a Bible for one happy Psalm and one sad one.

ACTIVITIES: **1. Musical Medley**

➤ In advance, get together **<u>short extracts</u>** from a variety of Christian music. Try to include contemporary songs and some which reflect the culture and background of your youngsters. If possible, also have some from different countries. ◄ Play them. Ask your group to talk about what they like and dislike. State clearly that God likes all sorts of music: He enjoys whatever people do to praise Him!

2. Musical Moods

➤ In advance, get together some simple musical instruments. <u>Alternatively</u>, have your youngsters make their own from any materials you can provide, (eg boxes, cartons, beans, elastic bands, string etc)! Also, think of some feelings, (eg happy, sad, angry, worried, sleepy etc), and write the words <u>and/or</u> draw a face to show each one on a separate piece of card. ◄ Now ask your youngsters to get into small groups. Give each group a different card. Ask each group to 'compose' a piece of music expressing the feeling on its card. Have an opportunity to hear everybody's ideas.

Extra: You may wish to use this series to introduce some contemporary worship songs: 'Praise Him on the Trumpet' would fit in well with this session.

KEY VERSE: *Let everything that breathes praise the Lord.* Psalm 150:6

Checklist

☐ ....
☐ ....
☐ ....
☐ ....
☐ ....
☐ ....

Date _____

Planning Notes

Things to
remember
for next
time...

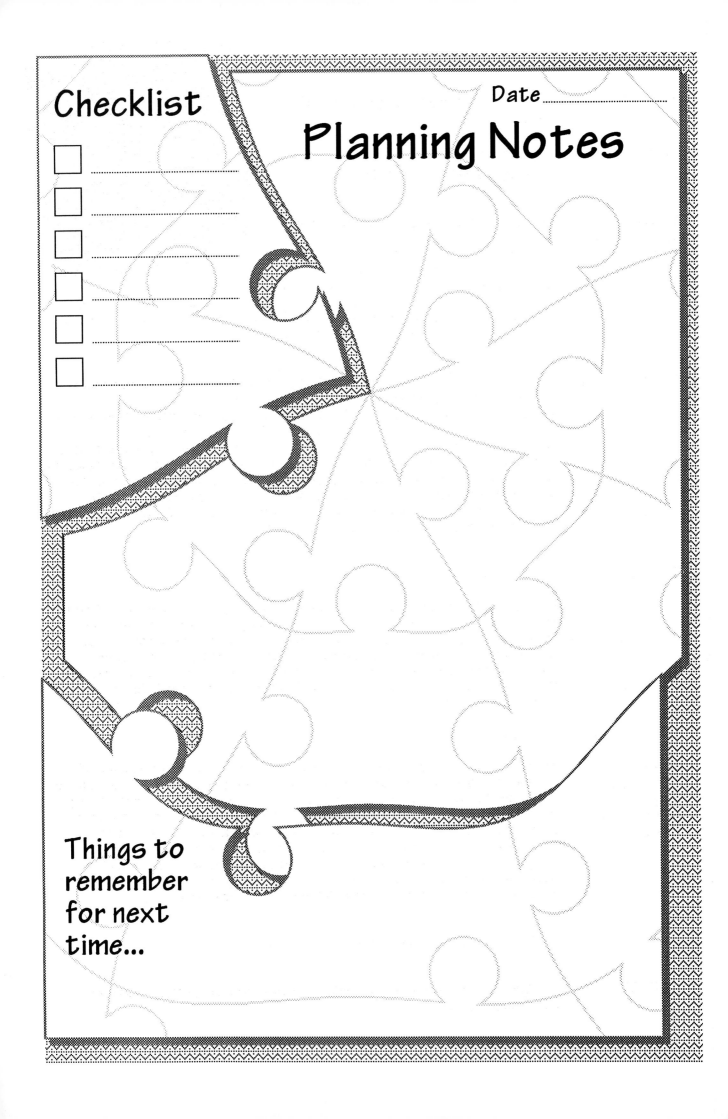

TITLE: ...For His Love

BIBLE BASE: Psalm 103 (Praise to the Lord of Love)

WE WANT OUR YOUNGSTERS TO...

... really know how great God's love is!

LEAD-IN:

[The answer to the last two questions is 'more than we can imagine!']

➤ In advance, make up about ten **simple** quiz questions on geography and measurement, (eg which is the biggest mountain in the world? etc). Make it fun! To help your youngsters, perhaps have several answers to choose from for some of the questions. Finish with: **how far is the sky above the earth?** and **how far is the east from the west?** ◄ Ask your youngsters to get into similar-sized teams. And do the quiz!

HOW TO START:

◆ ➤ If appropriate, write out *Psalm 103:6-18* on OHP <u>or</u> poster-sized paper in advance, so that everyone will be able to see it! ◄
◆ Ask your youngsters to listen for the last two questions from the LEAD-IN quiz somewhere in the poem - then have *Psalm 103:6-18* read aloud.
◆ <u>Either</u> altogether <u>or</u> in small groups, work out some simple signs and actions to go with lines of the Psalm, (eg right arm raised for 'the Lord', both hands on the heart for 'love' etc) - then re-read the verses, this time with the actions!
◆ Talk about it with questions such as: **what does this poem tell you about God? How much does God love those who respect Him? What does He do with the things we do wrong (called 'sins')?**

ACTIVITIES:

1. A Reminder...

Perhaps begin by going out and looking up to the sky - **this** is how great God's love is!! Then have your youngsters cut a cloud <u>or</u> sun <u>or</u> star from stiff paper <u>or</u> card. Have them decorate these shapes using any materials you can provide, (eg coloured pens, scraps of coloured paper and material etc). As appropriate, have your youngsters add 'God loves (their name)' and their favourite verse from the Psalm. Encourage everyone to keep these at home as a reminder of how much God loves them!

2. Compass Game

[Introduce more complex directions, such as north-north-east, for older youngsters!]

➤ In advance, cut lots of pieces of wool <u>or</u> string, each about 10cms long. ◄ Have all your youngsters stand together in the middle of a large room <u>or</u> outdoor area. Say that you are at the centre of a 'compass' and point out which wall <u>or</u> marker is north, which is south etc. Have a leader <u>or</u> helper at each 'compass point' if possible. Now ask your youngsters to get into equal-sized teams. Call out directions - sometimes one at a time, sometimes two (or more!) together! Give each of the first four youngsters to arrive at the 'compass point' a piece of wool. At the end of the game, have each team tie together **all** the pieces of wool its members have won: the team with the longest piece, wins!

Extra: 'God is Good' would fit in well with this session.

KEY VERSE: *As high as the sky is above the earth, so great is his love for those who respect him.* Psalm 103:11

Checklist

☐ ....

☐ ....

☐ ....

☐ ....

☐ ....

☐ ....

Date ....

Planning Notes

Things to remember for next time...

TITLE: ...When You're Guilty

BIBLE BASE: **Psalm 32** (It is Better to Confess Sin)

WE WANT OUR YOUNGSTERS TO...

... understand that we have all done wrong things - none of us is perfect!

... know that it feels good to own up to what you have done wrong and let God forgive you.

LEAD-IN:

➤ In advance, choose a short video clip <u>or</u> extract from a story in which someone does something wrong. ◄ Talk together about it. Ask: **which character(s) feel bad about what has happened?** Take a vote on who your youngsters think felt worst! Focus on the person who did the wrong thing, asking: **how do you think he/she feels?** Go on to talk about times when we do wrong things. Ask: **how do you feel when you have upset a friend or member of your family? Or when you have done something wrong?** Lead in by saying that there is a Psalm about this kind of situation...

HOW TO START:

[It may be appropriate to go on to a simple explanation of what Jesus did on the cross, perhaps using the 'bridge diagram' to help your youngsters understand.]

◆ ➤ If appropriate, write out *Psalm 32:1-11* on OHP <u>or</u> poster-sized paper in advance, so that everyone will be able to see it! ◄

◆ If possible, decide as a group on an appropriate rhythm background for a Psalm about this kind of guilty feeling, (eg fast and upbeat? soft or loud? etc) - have your youngsters make the rhythm as *Psalm 32:1-11* is read aloud.

◆ Talk about it with questions such as: **what does the songwriter say it feels like when you do not admit you have done wrong? What should you do if you want God to forgive you? What makes a person really happy?**

◆ As appropriate, have a short time of quiet for your youngsters to think about - and own up to - things they have done wrong...

ACTIVITIES:

1. Junk Race

➤ In advance, collect together all sorts of junk, (eg empty boxes and plastic bottles etc) - the bigger, the better! Also, think of about six really difficult but silly questions, (eg what colour socks did I wear last Tuesday? etc). ◄ Now ask for two volunteers to run a race. Ask them the questions first: give them a piece of junk for every wrong answer! Now have them run the race with all the junk they have 'won'!! Make a link with trying to live weighed down with the junk of wrong things we have not owned up to. As appropriate, state clearly how we can get rid of the 'junk'!

2. Affirmation Game

[You will need to supervise your youngsters whilst they are outside!]

If your youngsters have been taking this seriously, have an 'Affirmation Game', so that they go away feeling good about themselves. Have your youngsters get into groups of about six **with a leader in each group**. Ask one youngster from each group to leave the room. The rest of the group then decides on **three** good things to say about that person. He/she then returns to hear the comments - make absolutely sure that there are no negative ones! Do exactly the same for each person in the group.

Extra: 'I get so Excited, Lord' would fit in well with this session.

KEY VERSE: *Happy is the person whose sins are forgiven, whose wrongs are pardoned.*
                                                                    Psalm 32:1

Checklist

☐ ....

☐ ....

☐ ....

☐ ....

☐ ....

☐ ....

Date ....

Planning Notes

Things to
remember
for next
time...

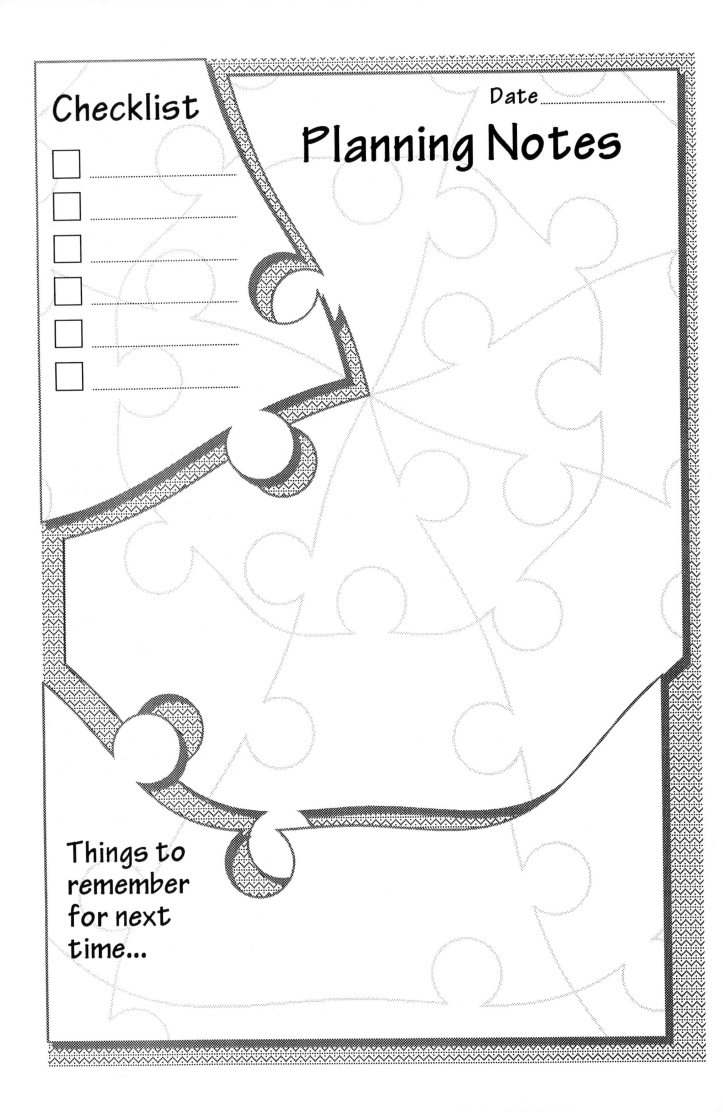

TITLE: ...Give Thanks!

BIBLE BASE: **Psalm 136:1-9 & 23-26** (God's Love Continues For Ever)

WE WANT OUR YOUNGSTERS TO...
... **realise how much we have to be thankful to God for!**

LEAD-IN: Have your youngsters sit in circles of about eight - make sure that there is a leader in each one! Get each person in turn to tell the others about the best thing that has happened to them in the week.

HOW TO START:
◆ ➤ If appropriate, write out *Psalm 136:1-9 & 23-26* on OHP <u>or</u> poster-sized paper in advance, so that everyone will be able to see it! ◄
◆ Ask your youngsters to suggest things which people should be grateful to God for - make a list of these as you go along.
◆ Have *Psalm 136:1-9 & 23-26* read aloud to the group - get your youngsters to join in with the *'His love continues for ever'* refrain each time.
◆ Ask your youngsters to say which verse means most to them.
◆ End by making up a Psalm following the pattern of *Psalm 136* - have your youngsters suggest verses, perhaps using ideas from the list you just made and the LEAD-IN. After each one, get everyone to join in with: *'His love continues for ever'*. If there are the right skills in the group, you might like to try rapping <u>or</u> developing a rhythm backing for this.

ACTIVITIES: **1. Poster Collage**

<u>Either</u> altogether <u>or</u> in small groups, have your youngsters make a large poster to illustrate *'Give thanks to the Lord because he is good'* <u>or</u> *'His love continues for ever'*: they could draw and colour <u>or</u> collage their own pictures <u>and/or</u> stick on words and images cut out of magazines.

2. Clapping Game

Have everyone sitting in a circle. Begin the rhythm: slap thighs, clap hands, click fingers (right hand), click fingers (left hand). When everyone has picked up the rhythm, stop and give everyone a number. You begin the game by saying your number followed by someone else's (during the finger-clicking part!) The person whose number you say must respond straightaway with their number and someone else's ...and so on. When someone makes a mistake, they become the biggest number and everyone moves around one place - the object of the game is to end up as number one!

Extra: 'Come on and Celebrate' would fit in well with this session.

KEY VERSE: *Give thanks to the Lord because he is good. His love continues for ever.*
Psalm 136:1

Checklist

- [ ] _____
- [ ] _____
- [ ] _____
- [ ] _____
- [ ] _____
- [ ] _____

Date _____

Planning Notes

Things to remember for next time...

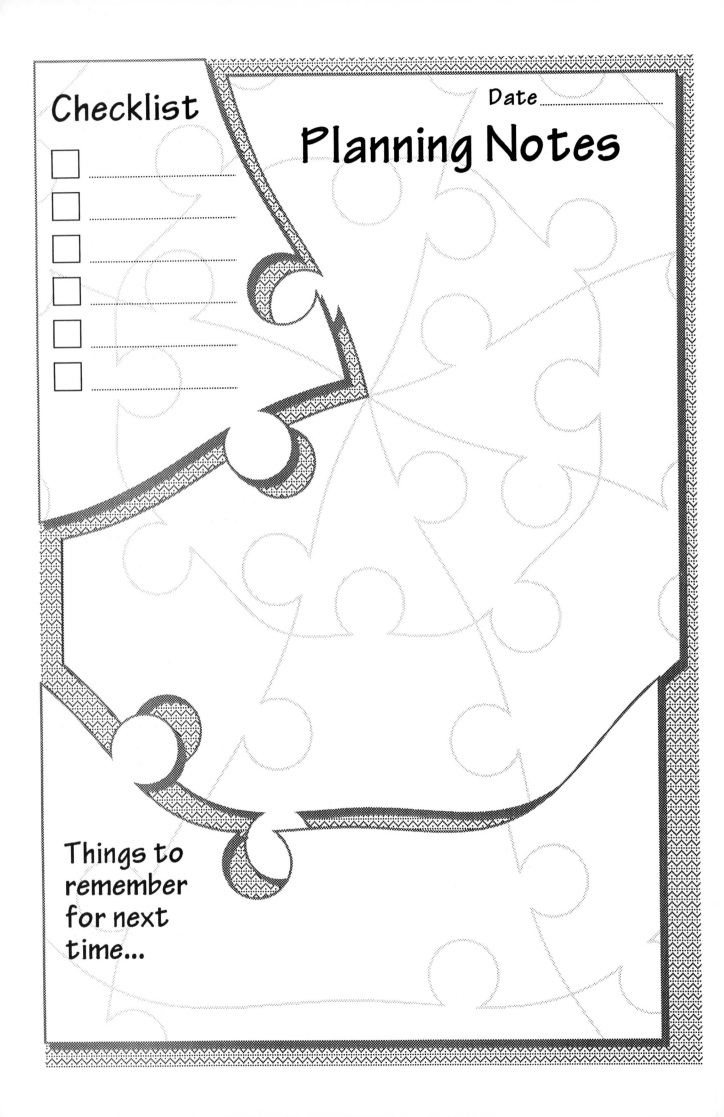

TITLE:	**A Disciple who Betrayed**

BIBLE BASE: **Matthew 26:1-5** (The Plan to Kill Jesus), **14-25** (Judas Becomes an Enemy of Jesus) **& 47-56** (Jesus is Arrested)

WE WANT OUR YOUNGSTERS TO...

... **become aware of all that Jesus went through for us: one of His closest friends betrayed Him.**

LEAD-IN:
[Make sure everyone knows what 'betrayed' means!]

➤ In advance, work out a scenario relevant to your youngsters which involves betrayal by a friend, (eg a group of bullies are out to find someone... one of his/her friends takes some money to lead the bullies to him/her...). ◄ Act it out. Talk together about the situation, with questions such as: **how do you think the betrayed person felt? Have you ever been in a situation like this?**

HOW TO START:
[It would add atmosphere to tell this story by candlelight!]

◆ ➤ The Passover meal would have consisted of unleavened bread, wine, bitter herbs, sauce and lamb... In advance, collect together as many objects to represent these as you can. ◄ Set them out before you begin and use them as you tell the story.

◆ Begin: *Judas had a secret... at least, he thought it was a secret. As he sat down to the special Passover festival supper with Jesus and the other disciples, he tried to act as if nothing was wrong at all. But Jesus knew everything...*

◆ Focus on how Jesus might have felt here: link in with the LEAD-IN, as appropriate.

ACTIVITIES:

1. 30 Pieces of Silver

➤ In advance, choose about eight objects from a catalogue which will appeal to your youngsters, (eg trainers, walkman etc). Cut out the pictures and make a note of the prices. Also, perhaps make some simple silver coins (from foil <u>or</u> milk bottle tops) to award as points! ◄ Ask your youngsters to get into small teams. Show the first picture and ask the teams to guess how much the object is worth. Award a point (<u>or</u> 'coin') for the nearest guess! Do the same with the other objects. The team with the most points at the end, wins! Go on to ask: **how much is a person worth?** Go on to talk about the 30 silver coins (about four months wages) Judas took for Jesus...

2. Easter Frieze - Part One!

You can do this project altogether as a whole group <u>or</u> in small groups <u>or</u> individually. Have a large strip of paper divided into four for each frieze. Have BETRAYED written in large letters at the top of the first section. Have your youngsters make a bag from cloth <u>or</u> paint one. Also make <u>or</u> paint some silver coins. As appropriate, add the KEY VERSE <u>or</u> a short prayer <u>or</u> invite your youngsters to write their own thoughts and reactions on paper and stick them to the first part of the frieze.

KEY VERSE:

He was hated and rejected by people. He had much pain and suffering.
Isaiah 53:3

Checklist

☐ ....
☐ ....
☐ ....
☐ ....
☐ ....
☐ ....

Date ....

Planning Notes

Things to
remember
for next
time...

TITLE: A Disciple who Deserted

BIBLE BASE: **Matthew 26:31-35** (Jesus' Followers will Leave Him) **& 69-75** (Peter Says He Doesn't Know Jesus)

WE WANT OUR YOUNGSTERS TO...

... become more aware of all that Jesus went through for us: one of His closest friends deserted Him;

... think about being loyal to their friends.

LEAD-IN: Have a game of 'Animal Families'! ➤ In advance, make a list of animals which make a distinctive noise - include cockerels! ◄ Whisper each different animal name to four youngsters: do this randomly, or the game will be too easy! When you say 'go', everyone moves around the room making the noise of their animal, listening for others making the same noise! The first 'animal family' to get together, wins! Repeat several times with different animals, but always include cockerels! Lead-in by saying that the sound of a cockerel once made someone feel very bad indeed...

HOW TO START: ◆ Begin: *Peter was hoping that all this was just a bad dream... When Jesus had talked before about suffering and dying, Peter and the other disciples had not really wanted to listen. But, as the soldiers took Jesus away, Peter had the most awful feeling... "Jesus really needs his friends to stand by him now", he thought to himself...*

◆ Ask: **why do you think Peter let Jesus down?**

◆ Talk together about how Jesus might have felt here...

ACTIVITIES: **1. A Loyal Friend?**

Ask your youngsters for examples of situations today in which it would be easy to desert a friend <u>or</u> God, as appropriate, (eg people laugh at you for coming to this club etc). Write the situations down as you go along. Now ask your youngsters to get into small groups. Then select one of the situations and turn it into the beginning of a story, (eg "You don't really believe all that rubbish, do you?" laughed Nicky. "If you ask me, anyone who believes in God needs their head looking at!" Jo just did not know what to say...) Ask the groups to draw <u>or</u> prepare to tell <u>or</u> act out what happens next. Have an opportunity to see/hear everyone's ideas. Help your youngsters talk about similar situations they have found/find themselves in: be understanding about the pressures, talk together about solutions - and pray!

2. Easter Frieze - Part Two!

Write DESERTED in large letters at the top of the second section. Have a large picture of a cockerel on show. Have your youngsters draw and paint a cockerel in the second section. Stick on real feathers, if possible! As appropriate, add the KEY VERSE <u>or</u> a short prayer, (eg 'Help me, Lord, to be loyal') <u>or</u> invite your youngsters to write their own thoughts and reactions on paper and stick them to the second part of the frieze.

KEY VERSE: *He was beaten down and punished, but he didn't say a word. He was like a lamb being led to be killed.* Isaiah 53:7

Checklist

- ☐ ....
- ☐ ....
- ☐ ....
- ☐ ....
- ☐ ....
- ☐ ....

Date _____

Planning Notes

Things to remember for next time...

TITLE: **Disciples who were Devoted**

BIBLE BASE: **John 19:16-42** (*from* Jesus is Crucified *to* Jesus is Buried)

WE WANT OUR YOUNGSTERS TO...
... **become more aware of all that Jesus went through for us;**
... **see that following Him will sometimes be sad and painful;**

LEAD-IN: ➤ In advance, make a list of about seven things which have to do with Easter, but are not part of the original story, (eg eggs, chocolate, bunnies etc)! Add the word 'cross' somewhere on your list. ◄ Ask your youngsters to get into teams of about six. Have one person from each team come forward and whisper the first word to them! They run back to their teams and draw the word <u>or</u> model it in plasticine <u>or</u> Blu-tack - no talking! When the team has guessed this word, another person runs for the second word - and so on. The first team to guess all the words, wins! Now ask: **which is the odd one out? Why?**

HOW TO START: ◆ ➤ In advance, collect together some simple visual aids for the story, (eg wood, nails, dice, vinegar, spices, cloth etc). ◄ Show them as you tell the story, perhaps from the women's perspective.
◆ Begin: *I still cannot believe what has happened. It only seems like yesterday that we were all with Jesus, being amazed at all He did and said. But now...?*
◆ As appropriate, use the visual props again to help your youngsters recall and re-tell the events <u>and/or</u> react to them.
◆ Focus on what was happening to Jesus... and clearly and simply say why.

ACTIVITIES:

[It may be good to have this game before the main teaching!]

1. Rescue Dodgeball

Ask your youngsters to get into two teams - A and B. Give team A two large, soft balls. Have team A stand along the sides of your meeting room and team B stand at one end. On the word 'go', all of team B runs to the other end of the room whilst team A throw the balls at them. When team B reach the other wall they are 'safe', but anyone who is hit by a ball has to stand still - he/she can be 'rescued' if a team mate risks running back to grab him/her. Do this eight times. Count how many team B members are still running free, then swap. Talk about rescue in this game and make a link with the teaching content, as appropriate!

2. Easter Frieze - Part Three!

Write EXECUTED in large letters at the top of the third section. Have your youngsters <u>either</u> paint <u>or</u> make a large cross <u>or</u> crown of thorns; <u>Or</u> paint the props from the story (<u>or</u> attach the actual props!) As appropriate, add the KEY VERSE <u>or</u> a short prayer, (eg 'Lord Jesus, thank you for your love') <u>or</u> invite your youngsters to write their own thoughts and reactions on paper and stick them to the third part of the frieze.

KEY VERSE: *...we are healed because of his wounds.* Isaiah 53:5

Checklist

☐ ....
☐ ....
☐ ....
☐ ....
☐ ....
☐ ....

Planning Notes

Things to
remember
for next
time...

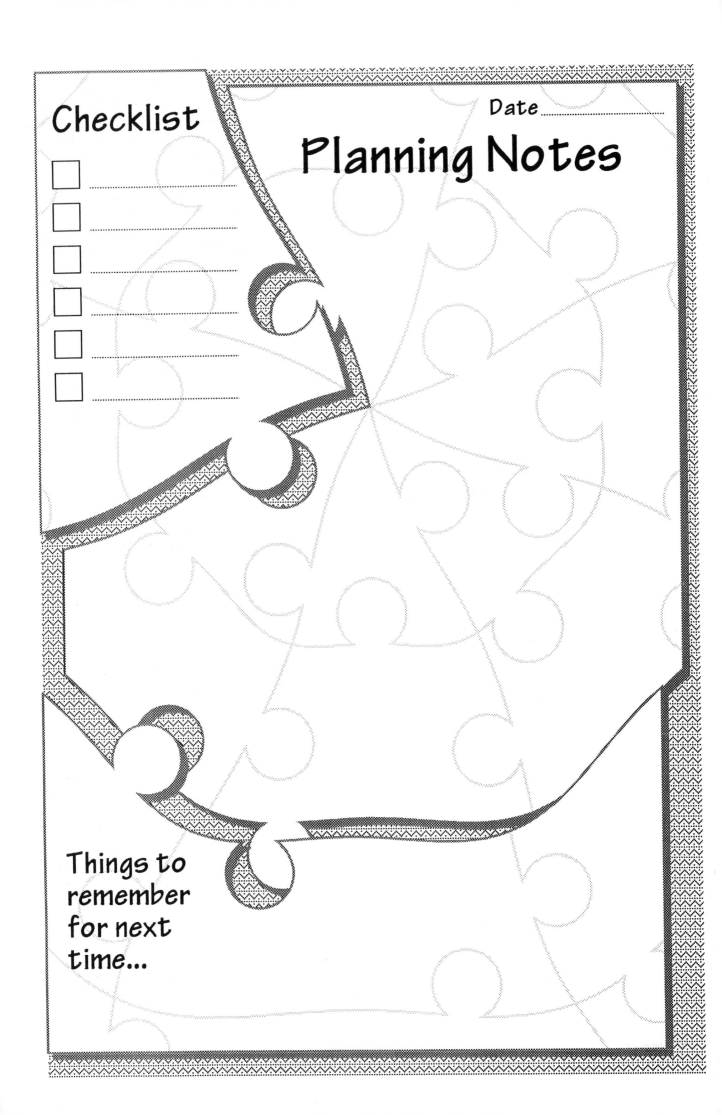

TITLE: **A Disciple who Doubted**

BIBLE BASE: John 20:19-29 (Jesus Appears to His Followers & Jesus Appears to Thomas)

WE WANT OUR YOUNGSTERS TO...
... know that Jesus came alive after death - and that there is proof of this!
... understand what this means for us today!

LEAD-IN: ➤ In advance, find about six little known facts or true stories - the more unusual, the better! Have evidence to back them up, (eg 'The Guiness Book of Records'). Now ask your youngsters to get into small groups. ◄ Read out the facts or stories one by one. After each one, ask your youngsters to decide whether it is TRUE or FALSE. Take a vote. Ask one or two youngsters **how** they chose each time. Ask some who chose FALSE: **how could I prove to you that this is TRUE?** Lead in by saying that the disciple in the story found it impossible to believe that what he was hearing was true...

HOW TO START:
◆ Begin: *Thomas looked hard at his friends. Just yesterday they were frightened and desperately sad... but now they were jumping for joy! "He's alive!" they laughed, "Jesus was dead, but now He's alive...!"*
◆ Perhaps your youngsters feel a bit like Thomas.... Ask: **what makes it difficult to believe that Jesus is alive now?**
◆ Talk simply about the 'evidence' that Jesus is alive in your own life...
◆ ...Give your youngsters an opportunity to respond for themselves.

ACTIVITIES:

1. Easter Frieze - Part Four!

Write ALIVE in large letters at the top of the final section. Have your youngsters either paint an empty tomb, perhaps adding real flowers and greenery to the garden; or paint the disciples celebrating, perhaps including pictures of themselves! As appropriate, add the KEY VERSE or a short prayer or invite your youngsters to write their own thoughts and reactions on paper and stick them to the final part of the frieze.

2. Easter Celebration!

Have a party to celebrate the fact that Jesus is alive today! Have simple food and/or games and/or music and/or simple decorations... anything you can provide would be great! Make sure that your youngsters are clear about the reason for the celebration!

KEY VERSE: *[He] will make many people right with God; he will carry away their sins.*
Isaiah 53:11

Checklist

☐ ....

☐ ....

☐ ....

☐ ....

☐ ....

☐ ....

Date ....

Planning Notes

Things to remember for next time...

TITLE: The Holy Spirit

BIBLE BASE: John 14:16-17; Acts 1:8;
Galatians 5:19-26

WE WANT OUR YOUNGSTERS TO...

... understand who the Holy Spirit is and
what He does;

... as appropriate, ask for more of Him in
their lives.

LEAD-IN: ➤ In advance, collect together some objects
which are useless if something is missing inside,
(eg a balloon with no air, pen with no ink, glove puppet with no hand, radio with
no batteries, carton with no drink etc). ◄ Put all the objects out on a tray - with
the something missing! Show them to your youngsters. Ask: **what do you
notice about all these things?** and, if necessary: **what is missing?**

HOW TO START: ◆ Get your youngsters' attention with a very short drama about a friend who is
going away, eg:
A: Well, goodbye. I'll really miss you when you've gone.
B: Yes, I'll miss you too. But don't be sad. I'll write to you, I promise. I'll
write every week. I won't forget...
◆ Begin: **When Jesus was going back to be with His Father in heaven, He
promised that He would not forget His disciples. He promised that He
would send the Holy Spirit...**
◆ Go on to explain that the Holy Spirit:
- is God's gift to us when we become Christians;
- is the part of God which lives in us;
- is God's power in us - without Him we are like the balloon with no air or the
pen with no ink!
- produces good things in our lives and makes us more like Jesus.
As appropriate, read the Bible verses which go with each point. Then pray!

ACTIVITIES: ### 1. Find the Fruit!

➤ In advance, cut nine simple fruit shapes out of paper <u>or</u> card. Write each fruit
of the Spirit from *Galatians 5:22-23* on a separate fruit shape. <u>Alternatively</u>, get
together and label some real fruit! Then **<u>carefully</u>** choose some of the wrong
things the sinful self does from *Galatians 5:19-21* - write them in words your
youngsters will understand on separate pieces of black paper <u>or</u> card, (eg being
angry, being selfish, making trouble etc). ◄ Hide them all around your meeting
room before anyone arrives. Have your youngsters search for them. Then
separate the fruit of the Spirit from the wrong things. If appropriate, arrange the
fruit of the Spirit on paper <u>or</u> a wall as a visual aid for the rest of the series.

2. Fruit 'Kebab'

➤ In advance, get together different kinds of fruit - fresh <u>and/or</u> tinned <u>and/or</u>
dried. Cut them into small pieces, as appropriate! ◄ Give each youngster a
cocktail stick. Invite them to choose some fruit to skewer onto it. Then eat and
enjoy it together!

KEY VERSE: *The Spirit produces the fruit of love, joy, peace, patience, kindness, goodness,
faithfulness, gentleness, self-control.* Galatians 5:22-23

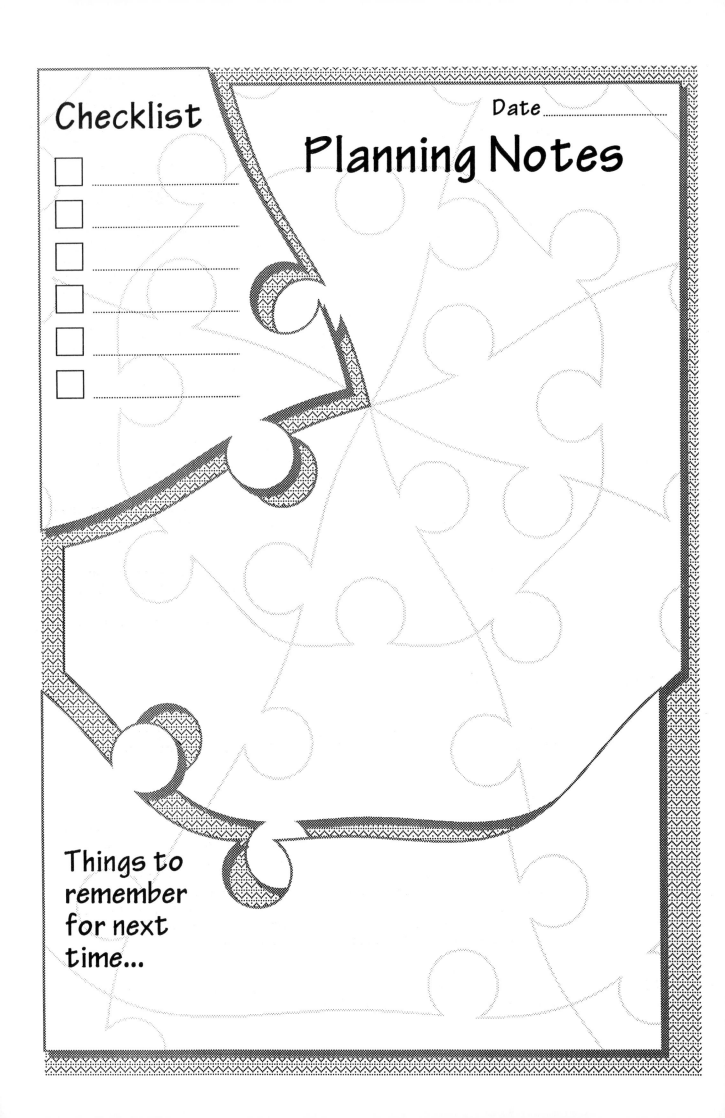

Checklist

☐ ....

☐ ....

☐ ....

☐ ....

☐ ....

☐ ....

Date ....

Planning Notes

Things to
remember
for next
time...

TITLE: Love

BIBLE BASE: **Hosea 1:1-3:5** (*from* Hosea's Wife and Children *to* Hosea Buys Back his Wife)

WE WANT OUR YOUNGSTERS TO...
... **understand that God's love is constant;**
... **consider how they can love others as He loves us - and ask for the Holy Spirit's help to do this.**

LEAD-IN:
➤ In advance, think of about six feelings people have towards each other, (eg 'I LOVE you', 'I HATE you', 'I am ANGRY with you', 'You make me SAD' etc). Write each one on a separate piece of paper. ◄ Put them face down in a pile. Now ask for a volunteer. Have him/her turn over the top piece of paper **without letting anyone else see!** Now ask him/her to mime that feeling! Have the rest of your group try to guess what the feeling is... Continue like this with the other five words.

HOW TO START:
[Don't get drawn into details... just say that Gomer had a bad reputation.]

◆ Ask your youngsters to get into small groups. Give each group a piece of paper, a pencil or pen and one of the feelings used in the LEAD-IN. Ask the groups to draw a simple face or picture which shows that feeling. Tack them all up on a board or wall as you tell the story.
◆ Begin: ***Nobody in the village could believe it! People giggled and gossiped as Hosea went by. "Did you know that Hosea is going to marry Gomer?!" "Never!! Hosea the holy man? Marry Gomer? Doesn't he know what she is like...?"***
◆ ...Stop the story at various points. Using the feelings pictures as appropriate, ask questions such as: **how do you think Hosea felt? What do you think he should do now?**
◆ Explain clearly, simply and briefly, how Hosea's love for his wife is a picture of God's love.

ACTIVITIES:

1. Celebrate!

Your youngsters may well be growing up with love which is inconsistent, unreliable, dependent on what they do and don't do... Have an opportunity for the constancy of God's love to really sink in with some **carefully selected** worship songs and prayers!

2. Live it Out!

➤ In advance, think of three situations relevant to your youngsters in which it is difficult to carry on loving someone, (eg a good friend spreads rumours about you, your brother takes your things etc). Give each situation to a helper, asking them to imagine that they are the person who has been hurt. ◄ Now ask your youngsters to get into small groups. Have each helper in turn explain their situation. Ask the groups to talk about what advice they would give. Have an opportunity to hear from each group. Talk clearly and sensitively about what might please God in each situation - but don't 'preach'!

KEY VERSE:
[Jesus said:] "I give you a new command: love each other. You must love each other as I have loved you." John 13:34

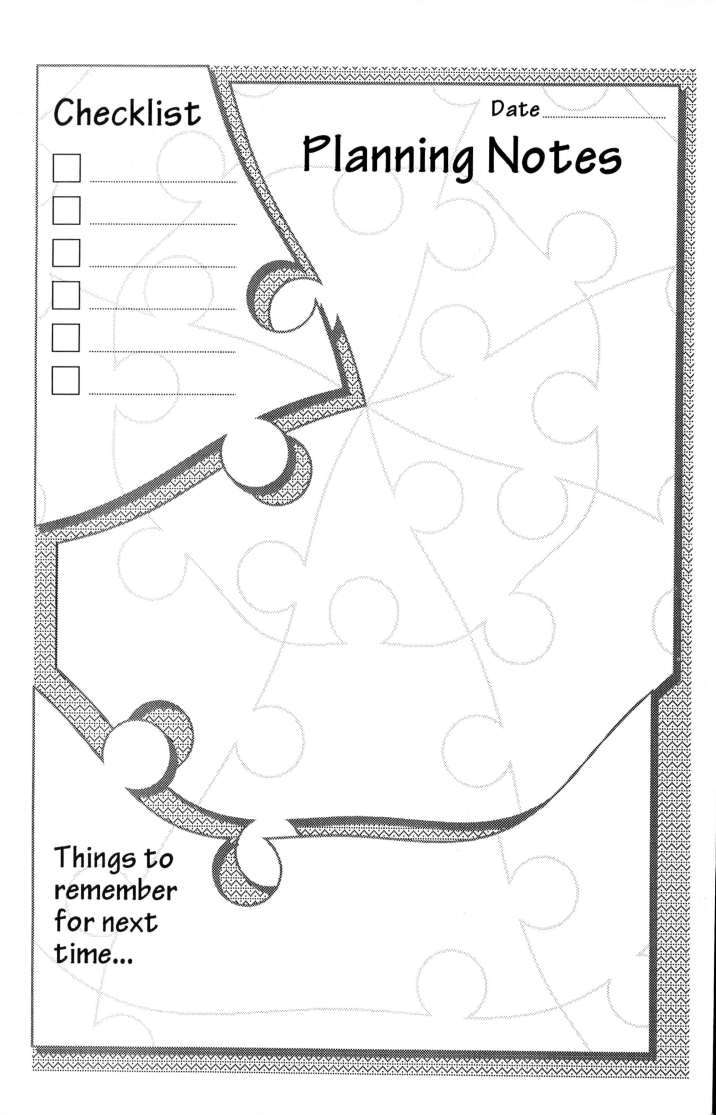

Checklist

- ☐ ....
- ☐ ....
- ☐ ....
- ☐ ....
- ☐ ....
- ☐ ....

Date ....

Planning Notes

Things to
remember
for next
time...

TITLE: Joy

BIBLE BASE: **Acts 16:16-34** (Paul and Silas in Jail)

WE WANT OUR YOUNGSTERS TO...
... **learn that God is a God of joy!**
... **be joyful!**

LEAD-IN:
➤ In advance, think of about five situations which your youngsters would really enjoy, (eg 'your favourite team wins the cup', 'you get a large gift' etc). Write each on a separate piece of paper. ◄ Give each situation to a pair of youngsters. Ask them to mime it. Everyone else must try to guess what is going on! Use this as a 'springboard' to talking about what makes us happy and how we show happiness, enjoyment, pleasure...

HOW TO START:
◆ Ask your youngsters to listen out for <u>three</u> people who were joyful - and <u>one</u> reason why! If appropriate, offer small prizes as an incentive and have '3 PEOPLE' and '1 REASON' written large as a reminder!
◆ Begin: **It was dark and cold in the jail. Rats and insects scuttled about in the dampness. The prisoners were cruelly treated: they were chained to a wall day in and day out, and often beaten. It was not a happy place to be in - so why were two of the prisoners singing...?**
◆ Highlight the fact that Paul, Silas and eventually the Jailer were joyful despite the circumstances... it was God who brought them joy!
◆ Help your youngsters see that the joy given by the Holy Spirit goes deeper than happiness! (Perhaps use the sea as an illustration: storms only affect the surface... underneath it is still calm.) Then pray!
◆ If appropriate, learn <u>or</u> listen to a contemporary song which rejoices in the Lord! Encourage your youngsters to join in with clapping, dancing, playing simple musical instruments etc.

ACTIVITIES:

1. Enjoy!

➤ In advance, organise something different (and memorable) which your youngsters will really enjoy! Possibilities include:
- Finding some suitable jokes to tell - encourage your youngsters to join in, but say clearly at the outset what you **don't** want to hear, (eg swearing, racism, sexual innuendo etc)!
- Showing a video;
- Organising a special event....◄

Make a link with the teaching content, as appropriate.

2. Dance!

Some Bible characters danced to express their joy! ➤ In advance, find an upbeat and joyful piece of music. It would also be good to invite someone with a real talent in for dance to lead this! ◄ Help your youngsters work out an appropriate dance routine in small groups. Have an opportunity to see everyone's ideas!

KEY VERSE: *Don't be sad, because the joy of the Lord will make you strong.* Nehemiah 8:10

Checklist

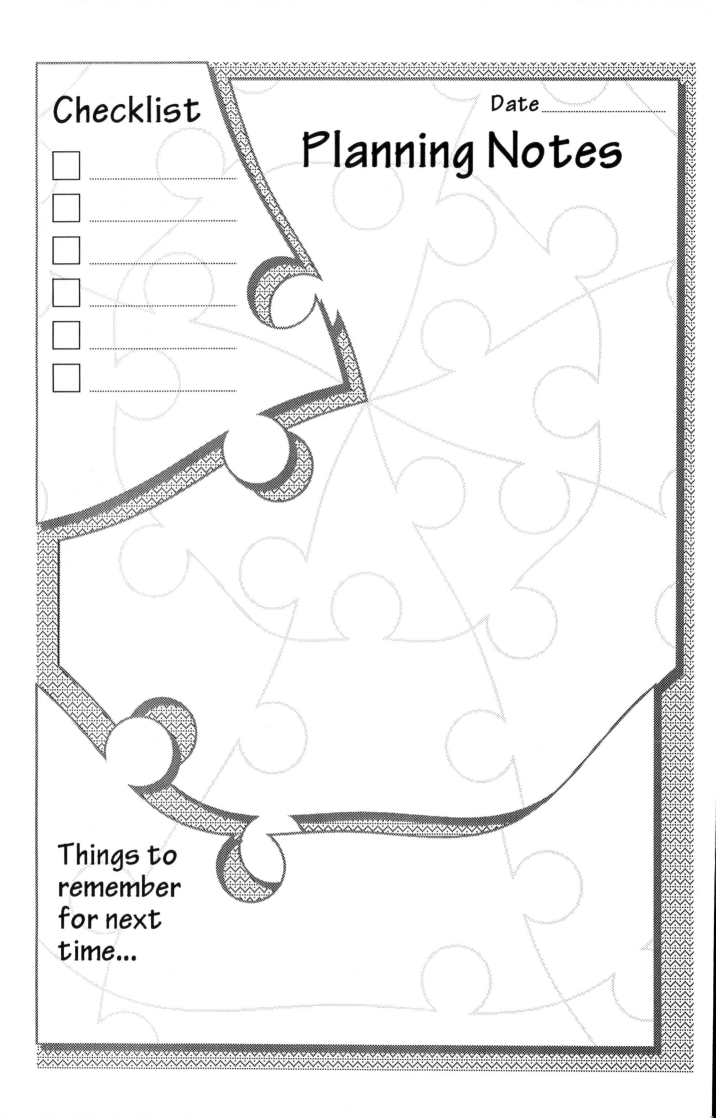

☐ _____
☐ _____
☐ _____
☐ _____
☐ _____
☐ _____

Date _____

Planning Notes

Things to remember for next time...

TITLE: Peace

BIBLE BASE: Mark 5:1-20 (A Man with Demons Inside Him)

WE WANT OUR YOUNGSTERS TO...
- ... know that Jesus has power over evil spirits;
- ... ask the Holy Spirit for peace.

LEAD-IN:

Ask for a volunteer and ask him/her to leave the room. Set up a simple obstacle course with whatever you have available, (eg chairs, boxes, people etc)! Also, ask all your youngsters to shout out wrong directions **when you give a signal**! Ask the volunteer to return and blindfold him/her. Begin guiding the volunteer round the course by shouting directions - then give the signal! Talk together about what happens. Lead in by explaining that a young man Jesus met was really confused by many evil spirits controlling him...

HOW TO START:

[Be careful how you deal with this... your youngsters may have had experience of a similar situation. Also, beware of frightening youngsters or of getting them interested in demon possession.]

- ◆ ➤ In advance, arrange for a leader to play the part of the young man **after** he had been healed by Jesus... ◄
- ◆ Begin: *"Look, there he is!", shouted someone form the crowd. Some people shook their heads sadly; some looked away in embarrassment; some were afraid; others laughed and joked as the young man ran out from among the graves...*
- ◆ ...Interview the leader playing the young man after the event - bring out how Jesus respected him and gave him peace!
- ◆ Then talk together about what makes us worry or feel confused and upset...
- ◆ ...Tell how the Holy Spirit has brought you peace in a particular situation.◆

As appropriate, pray together peace for each other. Perhaps also pray for peace in a war situation. And maybe try to have 30 seconds peace to finish...!

ACTIVITIES:

[You may need to make some templates for this in advance!]

1. Dove Mobile

Ask your youngsters if they know any symbols which stand for peace. Talk about the dove (which stands for peace **and** the Holy Spirit!) Give each youngster a piece of white card **or** stiff paper. Have them draw and cut out a dove shape.
Then give them a piece of white paper to fold like a concertina. Help them to make a slit in their dove and feed through the folded paper. Then fan it out to look like wings! Also add the KEY VERSE, if appropriate. Hang the dove up with a length of sewing cotton.

 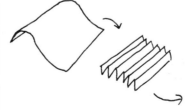 

cut hole in dove

2. Peace!

Give your youngsters a piece of paper and some paints <u>or</u> coloured pens <u>or</u> pencils. Ask them to paint peace! If appropriate, have an opportunity to see everyone's ideas. <u>Either</u> collect the paintings together to make a large picture <u>or</u> encourage your youngsters to keep them as a reminder of this part of the 'fruit'.

KEY VERSE:

Now may the Lord of peace give you peace at all times and in every way.
2 Thessalonians 3:16

Checklist

☐ ....
☐ ....
☐ ....
☐ ....
☐ ....
☐ ....

Planning Notes

Things to
remember
for next
time...

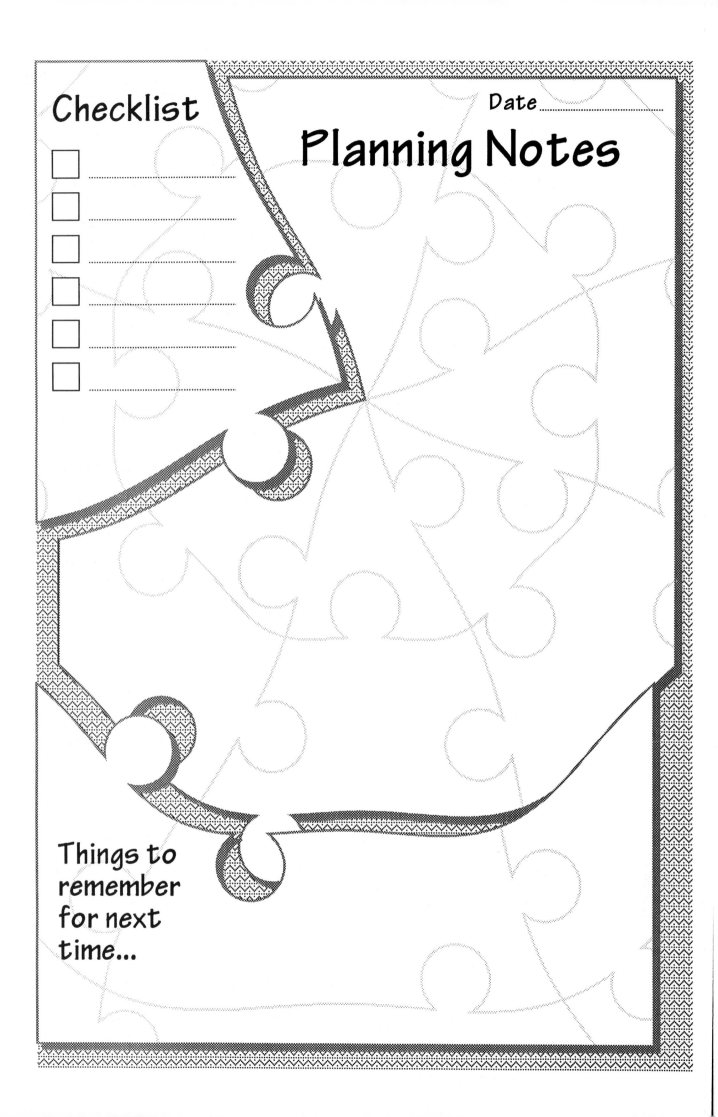

TITLE: Patience

BIBLE BASE: Job 1:1-2:13 (*from* Job, the Good Man *to* Job's Three Friends Come to Help)

WE WANT OUR YOUNGSTERS TO...

... **know that, even when everything goes wrong and seems unfair, God is still with us and still cares;**

... **learn to be patient - and ask for the Holy Spirit's help to do this.**

LEAD-IN: ➤ In advance, ask another leader to cheat during this! ◄ Plan and play one of your group's favourite games. See how your youngsters react to the cheating! Then talk together about other situations which are unfair.

HOW TO START:

[If you do say what happened in the end, avoid giving the impression that God always blesses those who suffer in this kind of way!]

◆ ➤ In advance, prepare a simple visual image for each of the things Job had at the beginning of the story, as described in *Job 1:3*. ◄

◆ Use these visuals to help your youngsters grasp how wealthy and happy Job was...

◆ Begin: *Job was the kind of man who seemed to have it all - a happy family, lovely children, servants to look after them, land stretching out as far as the eye could see...*

◆ ...Then take away the visuals one by one as you describe the disaster which befell Job.

◆ Ask: **did Job deserve what happened to him?** and then: **if you were Job, how would you have felt about God?**

◆ Say something like: *Things go wrong and are unfair in our lives too, but God never stops loving us and never stops caring. In difficult times like these we need to trust patiently in God like Job did...*

◆ ...Let your youngsters react to this for themselves - and pray!

ACTIVITIES:

1. It's Not Fair!

Have everyone think of situations in which innocent people are suffering - these could be personal <u>and/or</u> local <u>and/or</u> world-wide! Perhaps have groups of youngsters make up a newspaper headline <u>and/or</u> short article to go with each one, and collect them together to make a 'front page'. Talk together about the situations... but most of all, pray!

2. Hang On!

You will need a large playing area for this! Ask your youngsters to get into teams of six. Have the teams stand at one end of the playing area. Put a cone <u>or</u> other marker at equal distances from each team. When you say 'go', the first person from each team runs round the cone and back. He/she then grabs the hand of the second person, and they both run round the cone, holding hands all the time. They then grab the third person - and so on. The first team to have all six members run round together, wins! Point out how easy it was to let go of someone's hand: go on to say that God **never** lets go of us...

KEY VERSE: *Nothing (...) will ever be able to separate us from the love of God that is in Christ Jesus.* Romans 8:39

Checklist

- ☐ ....
- ☐ ....
- ☐ ....
- ☐ ....
- ☐ ....
- ☐ ....

Date ....

Planning Notes

Things to remember for next time...

TITLE: Kindness

BIBLE BASE: Jeremiah 38:1-13 (Jeremiah is Thrown into a Well)

WE WANT OUR YOUNGSTERS TO...

... know that God is kind;
... consider how they can show practical kindness to others - and ask for the Holy Spirit's help to do this.

LEAD-IN: Have a game of 'Corner Colours'! Stick a different coloured piece of paper in each corner of your meeting room (or on posts, if you are playing outside). Now ask your youngsters to get into teams of about six. Shout out a colour order, (eg 'blue, green, red, yellow!') - the first person in each team runs and touches the corners **in that order**. Shout out a different colour order for the second person... and so on. For the last person, shout out a long list of colours which will be impossible to remember! Stop after a short while. Ask: **why did I stop this?** Draw out the idea that you were being kind to the last runners!

HOW TO START:
◆ Begin: *"Jeremiah has really done it this time," complained the officers bitterly. "Have you heard what he has been telling people now?" As a prophet, Jeremiah's job was to pass on messages from God. Jeremiah knew that he had to keep speaking the truth, even though it made people angry - so angry that they wanted him out of the way...*
◆ Perhaps act this out: make a circle of chairs to represent a well and throw in a leader! Ask your youngsters for ideas of how to rescue him/her, then act out Ebed-Melech's solution!
◆ Bring out how kind Ebed-Melech was, especially in providing pads for Jeremiah's arms!

ACTIVITIES:

1. Brainstorm!

Ask your youngsters to get into groups of about six. Make sure that there is someone who is happy to write in each group. Give each group a large piece of paper and a thick pen. Ask: **how can we be kind at home?** Allow about one minute for the groups to think of and note down ideas. Then do the same with two or three other situations, (eg at school, in our neighbourhood etc). Keep it fast-moving! Finish with: **how can we be kind here in our club?** and maybe: **how can the leaders be kind?** Have an opportunity to look together at all the ideas. As appropriate, ask your youngsters to commit themselves to actually putting some of the ideas into practice - and pray!

2. Beware the Wolf!

Ask everyone to sit in a circle. Ask for a volunteer - the 'shepherd' - to leave the room. In his/her absence, choose another volunteer to be the 'wolf'! The rest of your group are 'sheep'! Ask the 'shepherd' to return and stand in the middle of the circle. The 'wolf' then 'kills' as many of the 'sheep' as he/she can by winking at them... the 'shepherd' must stop the 'wolf' by finding out who he/she is! Have about three games. Finally, have leaders be the 'shepherd' and the 'wolf'. This time, the 'shepherd' takes all the winks and no 'sheep' are 'killed'. Use this as an illustration of Jesus' kindness in dying for us...

KEY VERSE: *Be kind and loving to each other...* Ephesians 4:32

Checklist

- [ ]
- [ ]
- [ ]
- [ ]
- [ ]
- [ ]

Date _____

Planning Notes

Things to
remember
for next
time...

TITLE: Goodness

BIBLE BASE: 1 Samuel 20:1-42 (Jonathan Helps David)

WE WANT OUR YOUNGSTERS TO...
        ... know that God is good!
        ... consider how they can be good
            themselves - and ask for the Holy
            Spirit's help to do this!

LEAD-IN: Show two fruits - one good and fresh, the other
bad and mouldy! Ask your youngsters which one
they would like to eat! Share out the good fruit. Then ask: **this <u>fruit</u> is good,
but what does it mean to say that a <u>person</u> is good?** Look out for and check
the attitude that it's bad to be good (because it's 'creepy', less fun etc)! Lead in
by asking your youngsters to look for what was good about Jonathan...

HOW TO START: ◆ Present this story as a drama, with youngsters <u>and/or</u> other leaders playing
the different characters. ➤ You could record it onto tape in advance ◀ and
play it at your session!
        ◆ Begin:
        *DAVID: What have I done wrong, Jonathan? Why is your father still out to
        kill me?*
        *JONATHAN: Kill you? No! That's not true! My father, the king, tells me
        everything he is going to do! If he wanted to kill you, I would know about
        it...*
        *DAVID: Jonathan, don't you see? The king knows that you and I are
        friends. He won't tell you, because he knows that you will warn me...!*

ACTIVITIES: **1. Thinking This Through...**

        ➤ In advance, make up some kind of puzzle, (eg wordsearch, coded message,
        words hidden around the walls etc) containing the things which were good about
        Jonathan: LOYAL FRIEND, RESPECTS GOD, KEEPS PROMISES, DOES RIGHT, ANGRY
        AT WRONG, UNSELFISH... ◀ Have your youngsters do the puzzle in pairs or
        threes. Then ask them to get into small groups. Ask each group to choose **one**
        of the good things and make up a short drama to show it in action! Have an
        opportunity to see and talk about each group's drama. Finish with prayer, as
        appropriate.

        2. Take Aim!

*[Make sure that you
think this out carefully
and have it well
supervised!]*

Could your youngsters have clearly given the 'secret sign' like Jonathan did? Make
simple bows and arrows together - <u>or</u> provide them. Then have a competition to
see who can shoot them most accurately! <u>Alternatively</u>, have a game of darts <u>or</u>
any accuracy game!

KEY VERSE: *Surely your love and goodness will be with me all my life.* Psalm 23:6

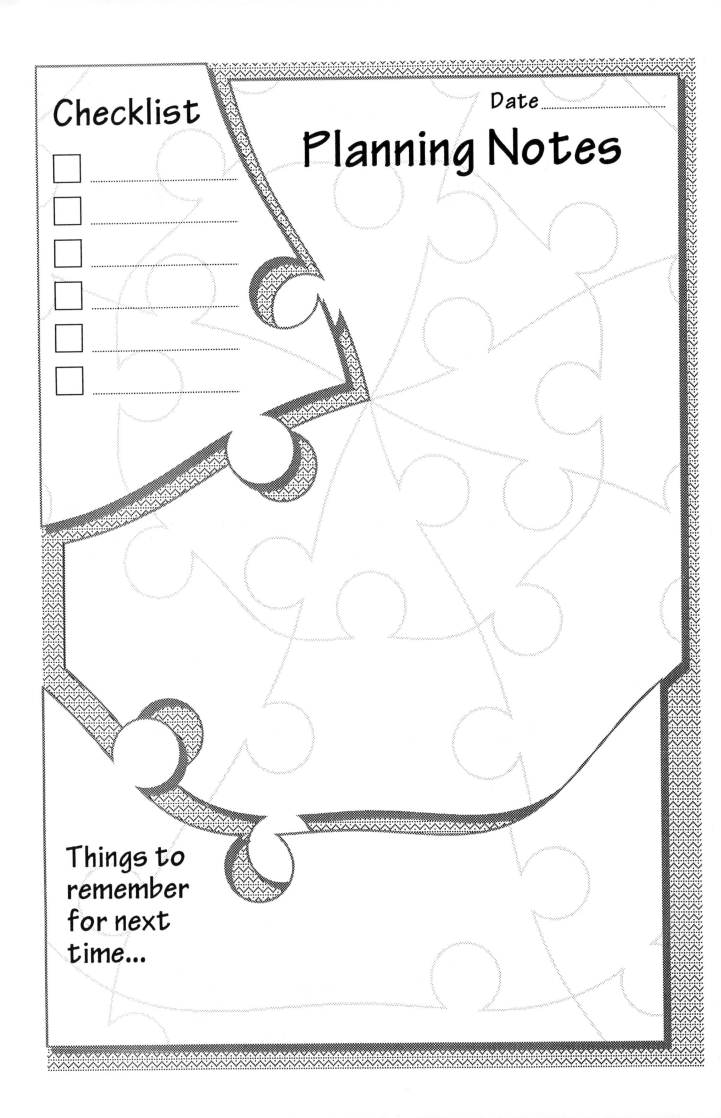

Checklist

☐ ....
☐ ....
☐ ....
☐ ....
☐ ....
☐ ....

Date ....

Planning Notes

Things to
remember
for next
time...

TITLE: Faithfulness

BIBLE BASE: 1 Kings 18:16-40 (Elijah and the Prophets of Baal)

WE WANT OUR YOUNGSTERS TO...

... know that God will never let us down;

... consider how they can be faithful to others and to God (as appropriate) - and ask for the Holy Spirit's help to do this.

LEAD-IN:

➤ In advance, think of about eight simple quiz questions about fire, (eg how do you contact the Fire Brigade in an emergency? etc). Also, get a piece of cloth, some water and a box of matches! ◄ <u>Either</u> run the quiz in teams <u>or</u> altogether, just for fun! For your last question, soak the cloth with the water and ask: **what would happen if I held a lighted match to this?** Use this question to bring out the fact that wet things do not catch fire!

HOW TO START:

◆ Get everybody to act out the story. Have individual youngsters <u>and/or</u> leaders play ELIJAH, KING AHAB and BAAL'S CHIEF PROPHET. Divide the rest of the group in two - one half play the PROPHETS OF BAAL and the other half the PEOPLE. If you can do this outside and include props, (eg wood, stones, water etc), so much the better!

◆ Begin: *People just left what they were doing and hurried up the hill. The huge crowd waited, wondering what was going to happen. Then Elijah stood up to speak: "It's time to make up your minds", he shouted, "If Baal really is god, follow him... but if the Lord is the true God, you should <u>only</u> worship Him..."*

◆ Bring out how faithful Elijah was to God - and how faithful God was to Elijah!

ACTIVITIES:

[Make sure you choose people who will appeal to your youngsters!]

1. Faithful Followers

Help your youngsters discover more about what it means to be faithful from the lives of other Christians. Possibilities include:

- Telling an exciting life story <u>or</u> showing a film version;
- Inviting someone to speak <u>and/or</u> be interviewed;
- Organising a mini-project: ask your youngsters to get into groups. Give each group information about a faithful Christian. Ask each group to use it to prepare a short drama <u>or</u> visual presentation for everyone else.

Whatever you choose, help your youngsters see how they can follow these examples in their own lives. Then pray!

2. Wax Pictures

Give each youngster a smallish piece of stiff paper <u>or</u> card. Have them colour bands of yellow, orange and red wax crayon until they have completely covered their piece of paper. Then have them paint over it all with black paint! Once it is dry, your youngsters can begin to scrape away flame shapes using a blunt pencil <u>or</u> something similar. Ask them to add some appropriate words (such as the KEY VERSE), if you wish.

scrape away design

paint black

KEY VERSE: *God (...) is faithful.* 1 Corinthians 1:9

Checklist

☐ ....
☐ ....
☐ ....
☐ ....
☐ ....
☐ ....

Date ....

Planning Notes

Things to remember for next time...

TITLE: Gentleness

BIBLE BASE: 1 Kings 19:1-18 (Elijah Runs Away);
Proverbs 15:1,4 & 25:15

WE WANT OUR YOUNGSTERS TO...

... see gentleness as a strength, not a
weakness!
... know that God is gentle with us;
... consider how they can be gentle - and
ask for the Holy Spirit's help to do this.

LEAD-IN: ➤ In advance, think of about ten questions on the
story from last session. Also, think of a false answer for each question. ◄ Have
everyone stand in the middle of your meeting room. Read out the first question
and the two answers: ask your youngsters to run to the left if they think the first
answer is correct and to the right if they think the second answer is correct. Say
which one is correct! Do the same with the other questions.

HOW TO START:

*[It would be good to
have taped sound
effects of the wind,
fire etc!]*

◆ ➤ In advance, find two objects: one which you can handle roughly, and one
you need to be gentle with, (eg an egg shell). ◄ Have all your youngsters (or
just a few volunteers) handle the objects. Use this as a 'springboard' to talk
about what it means to be gentle.

◆ ➤ In advance, also think of two gestures: one meaning good and one
meaning bad, (eg thumbs up, thumbs down). ◄ Ask your youngsters to use
the 'good' one when someone is gentle, and the 'bad' one when someone is
not! Stop the story whenever your youngsters use the gesture and get them to
say why.

◆ Begin: *How fast can you run? And how far can you run? After Elijah
defeated the prophets of Baal with God's strength, you'd think he would
feel confident and strong: But something scared him so much that he ran
and ran as fast as he could...*

◆ Focus on the fact that God is all-powerful - and yet very gentle!

ACTIVITIES:

*[You could also include
the KEY VERSE in this.]*

1. The Power of Gentleness

➤ In advance, think of about five quotes and/or well-known sayings. Add the
three Proverbs from the BIBLE BASE. Write each quote and/or saying out large on
a separate piece of paper, but miss out one or two key words from each. ◄ Show
and read them out, one by one, and have your youngsters guess the missing
words - you can either do this altogether, just for fun, or as a team game! Then
talk briefly about all the quotes and sayings, asking: **what do they mean? Are
they good advice?** Focus on the Proverbs: encourage your youngsters to think
about real-life situations in which a 'gentle word' might be more effective then an
angry one! And pray!

2. Modelling

Have your youngsters make a model of something gentle from whatever materials
you can provide. Perhaps suggest they make something which is powerful but
gentle, (eg a whale). (As appropriate, perhaps point out how your youngsters
need to be gentle with what they are making!)

KEY VERSE: *Let everyone see that you are gentle and kind.* Philippians 4:5

Checklist

- ☐ ....
- ☐ ....
- ☐ ....
- ☐ ....
- ☐ ....
- ☐ ....

Date ....

Planning Notes

Things to remember for next time...

TITLE: Self-control

BIBLE BASE: Matthew 4:1-11 (The Temptation of Jesus)

WE WANT OUR YOUNGSTERS TO...

- ... **see clearly that Jesus knows what it's like to be tempted;**
- ... **understand that He did not give in;**
- ... **recognise times when they are tempted to do wrong - and ask for the Holy Spirit's help not to give in.**

LEAD-IN:

[Don't pretend you did not notice those who took a sweet... but don't make an issue of it either!]

Before your youngsters arrive, put out a dish of sweets where everyone can see them. Add a sign which says: 'Don't eat these yet!'. Make sure that no leaders hover nearby, but keep an eye on what happens! Talk together about this with questions such as: **what was it like to see the sweets but know you should not have one? Can you think of other times when you have been tempted to do something you know you really should not do?**

HOW TO START:

- ◆ Help your youngsters imagine what it might feel like to be in a desert... and then not to eat a thing for 40 days!
- ◆ Begin: *Jesus must have been so hungry and so exhausted! When the devil came to tempt Him, He still knew how to be strong against the temptation - with the help of God's Word...!*

ACTIVITIES:

1. Balloon Volleyball

Ask your youngsters to suggest things which they are sometimes tempted to do which they know are wrong. Write each one on a separate balloon. Then blow the balloons up! Now ask your youngsters to get into two teams. Have the teams stand at opposite sides of a volleyball net <u>or</u> line of chairs <u>or</u> rope held by two leaders. Now divide the balloons between each team. On the word 'go', all the players try to bat the balloons over the net using their hands. Stop the game after about three minutes. The team with the <u>**least**</u> number of balloons over its side of the net, wins! As appropriate, use this to lead into a discussion of how we can <u>**really**</u> fight off temptation - then pop the balloons and pray!

2. Help!

➤ In advance, think of a number of situations in which there is a temptation to be overcome - make sure that they are all relevant to your youngsters! Write each one out as a 'problem page'-type letter. ◄ Ask your youngsters to get into small groups. Give each group a different 'letter'. Ask all the groups to work out (but not necessarily write!) a short reply. Have an opportunity to hear from each group. As appropriate, leave space for your youngsters to talk <u>and/or</u> pray quietly about real situations they face...

KEY VERSE:

When you are tempted, God will also give you a way to escape.
1 Corinthians 10:13

Checklist

☐ _____

☐ _____

☐ _____

☐ _____

☐ _____

☐ _____

Date _____

Planning Notes

Things to
remember
for next
time...

More Teaching Resources from Crusaders which:

- are Bible-based;
- will help you present clearly the challenges of living as a disciple in the 1990's;
- are particularly geared to outreach situations;
- contain clear teaching outlines for a whole series of sessions;
- help you 'tell the story' creatively;
- use a whole range of learning activities appropriate to the age bracket to get group members involved right from the outset!
- include photocopiable activity sheets;
- are flexible and easy-to-use;
- save you time!

FOR THE *7 TO 11*'S...

KEYS TO THE KINGDOM

7 sessions based on the idea that Jesus' parables are like treasure chests... if we have the keys to 'unlock' them, we will find a wealth of truths inside!

'...Lots of different ideas to modify... It was great to have such a choice... The ideas are all there for you.' Group Leader, Bristol.

PRICE: £5.50 (£4.25 to Crusader affiliates)   ISBN 1 897987 04 8

FOR THE *11 TO 14*'S...

ENCOUNTERS OF A LIFETIME

9 sessions based on a TV 'magazine style' format, focusing on people who met with Jesus... and on those who still meet with him today! The 'audience' will see clearly what each encounter shows us about Jesus and how they can meet Him themselves!

'...versatile and has a wide spectrum appeal. There is plenty of flexibility and it is easy to tailor the material to our needs. The dramas have been good fun and they have made our youngsters think and react.' Beth Tidmarsh, Group Leader, North London.

PRICE: £6.35 (£4.75 to Crusader affiliates)   ISBN 1897987 12 9

FIRST STEPS - MOVING FORWARD

6 sessions of essential teaching for young people starting out on the Christian life... and for those still thinking about it! The series is based on the parallels between human birth and being 'born again' as a Christian.

PRICE: £5.50 (£4.25 to Crusader affiliates)   ISBN 1 897987 09 9

WHAT'S IN IT FOR ME?

10 sessions to help young people discover God's Word for themselves! With its flexible, 'hands-on' approach, this material can be used where group members have no Bible knowledge... and also where they have heard it all before but just need encouragement to put it into practice!

'We have started the term with this and it is going down a storm! The kids love it - even some of our more difficult groups are really getting in to it... I have found the material easy-to-use, well laid out and effective in getting the point over.' Peter Walkinshaw, Schools Worker, Cumbria.

PRICE: £5.50 (£4.25 to Crusader affiliates)   ISBN 1 897987 05 6